397

HIDDEN GEMS AND HOMETOWN
FAVOURITES IN CANADA AND BEYOND

YOU
GOTTA
GO
HERE!

JOHN CATUCCI AND
MICHAEL VLESSIDES

Collins

You Gotta Go Here!

Copyright © 2017 by Lone Eagle Entertainment Ltd.

All rights reserved.

Published by Collins,

an imprint of HarperCollins Publishers Ltd

First edition

HarperCollins books may be purchased for educational, business, or sales promotional use through our Special Markets Department.

HarperCollins Publishers Ltd

2 Bloor Street East, 20th Floor

Toronto, Ontario, Canada

M4W 1A8

www.harpercollins.ca

Library and Archives Canada Cataloguing in Publication information is available upon request.

ISBN 978-1-44345-404-9

Printed and bound in Canada

QUAD 9 8 7 6 5 4 3 2 1

A NOTE TO THE READER

We hope this book provides much joy and a road map to your next great adventure (whether it's across the country or down the street). However, before heading out to a restaurant or attraction, always make sure to check if they are open and have what you want. Restaurants sometimes change locations or even close. Sometimes chefs leave and new ones arrive, bringing fresh, new menus with them. Dishes that are featured in this book may no longer be available (although they sure were delicious when we were there visiting). Have fun!

CONTENTS

CANADA

WESTERN CANADA

CENTRAL CANADA

This Tundra Buggy stands well above the 11 feet a polar bear can reach on its hind legs.

They may look slow and lumbering, but polar bears can hit top speeds of almost 20 mph! Remember to always have someone slower than you in the group.

Ahh, Ireland. I love your rolling hills and hidden lakes, but what I really crave is your mashed potato–hash brown hybrid, boxty.

Ciao! See what happens to my face when we get a few days off?

Introduction

Travel. For many of us, it's the end zone, the goal line, the checkered flag. It's where we want to end up someday, the reward for years of hard work, a respite from busy lives.

"When I retire, I'm going to travel."

"I'm going to take a year off from school to travel."

"Hey, how was your holiday?" "Amazing! We visited [whatever exotic destination your buddy actually went to]*."*

Not surprisingly, the travel industry is big business. Back in 2013, *Forbes* magazine noted that more than a *trillion* dollars was spent on travel worldwide—in the previous year alone! And travel has only gained in popularity since then. Think of all the websites, businesses, TV shows, and books (including this one!) dedicated to travel. It's huge.

For good reason, too. Simply put, travel is freakin' amazing. I mean, few things can compare with the sheer joy and exhilaration of packing your suitcase or backpack and heading off into the great unknown. Travel affords us the opportunity to see exotic places, meet new people with different ways of looking at the world, and (best of all!) try different kinds of food. It's not just for single people, either. Travelling as a family is easier and more affordable than ever.

That wasn't the case when I was a kid, especially for working-class families like mine. Money was tight in the Catucci household. In fact, the first overseas vacation we ever had was cut short by tragedy. When I was four years old, my parents decided to take me to Italy for a month. My *nonna* (grandmother) and aunt came to the airport to see us off. My aunt later recounted the chilling tale: As we boarded the plane, my *nonna* turned to her and said, "That's the last time I'll ever see them." Nonna died the next day.

I remember being in Italy, sitting on someone's kitchen counter, when the news of my *nonna*'s death arrived. It was the first time I ever saw my father cry. Needless to say, we cut our trip short and went home. Luckily, we travelled back to Italy eight years later. That was the last family trip we ever took.

Man, how things have changed. Now I make my living by travelling to far-flung destinations both here in Canada and abroad. In five years of shooting *You Gotta Eat Here!*, I've not only covered every province and all but one territory, but also spent time in the United States, England, Ireland, and Italy. And every step of the way has been incredible. As I always say, I have the best job in the world. And I do.

Yet there's some irony in all my travelling: I don't get to share it with my family. Not in person, that is. You see, even though I would love to have my wife and our two daughters accompany me on my trips, most of my travels are with the *You Gotta Eat Here!* crew: our director, Jim Morrison; director of photography, Steve Lindsay; sound man, Scott Chappel; camera assistant, Josh Henderson; and field producer, Sarah Cutts. So, for now, I share my adventures with my kids through stories and conversation. I did buy them an atlas, so now when I check in with them at night they flip through it to see where Dad is at the moment. It's not the same as holding their hands as we walk through London, but it helps ease the pain of being away from home so often.

If spending three-quarters of the year on the road has been a bit difficult, it's a challenge tempered by the education I've gotten and experiences I've had. There've been some very valuable lessons along the way, some obvious, some not so much.

LESSON #1: Canada Is Massive

Did you really need me to tell you that? Okay, so we all know what the textbooks tell us: Canada has the second-largest land mass of any country on earth. But it's not until you start travelling this amazingly diverse country that you realize exactly what that means. Take my home province of Ontario, for example. Yes, you can fit Italy *inside it*. It's that big. But let's put it in a practical context: To drive from my hometown of Toronto to Vermilion Bay (where we visited Buster's BBQ in Season 1) takes *twenty hours* . . . and you're still in the same province!

LESSON #2: Food Is the International Language

Whether it's Canada, the United States, Italy, England, or Ireland, we all speak the common language of food. We love talking about it, thinking about it, shopping for it, preparing it, smelling it, and eating it. Sure, we all put different things *in* our food, but that's what makes the world interesting, isn't it? (And thank goodness we all like pizza . . .)

LESSON #3: Canada Humbles You with Size, Europe Humbles You with Age

Canada turns 150 years old in 2017! *Woohoo!*

As exciting as that is to, oh, about 35 million humans, there are *people* in Europe older than Canada. Actually, that statement is not backed up by fact. Come to think of it, 150 is *really* old for a person. But in terms of Europe, it's just a drop in the bucket.

I think that's what I love most about Europe. Almost everywhere you go, you *feel* the history under your feet. Oh, this café is in a 3000-year-old building? Well *that* certainly gives a sense of history—and reminds us just how small we are in the grand scheme of things.

LESSON #4: The Key to Any Great Recipe Is Love

This might sound strange coming from a guy who samples food for a living, but anybody can make a burger. Just mush some ground beef into a patty, throw it in the frying pan, and a few minutes later . . . voila! Burger.

What separates that kind of meal from the kind that resonates in both your stomach and your memory is love. I can't tell what it tastes like, but you sure know it when you bite into it. Whether it's Frank's Pizza House in Toronto or Neighbour's Restaurant in Vancouver, love is the difference between someone's job and someone's life.

Come take a journey with me and the crew across Canada, with a few stops for good measure in the US and across the Atlantic. I hope you find your travels much like I find mine: They taste good, they smell sweet, and they feel wonderful.

CANADA

Oh, Canada. I owe you an apology.

You see, until I started hosting *You Gotta Eat Here!*, I forgot just how awe-inspiring you can be. I fell into the same trap that affects so many of our fellow Canucks: I believed that going away was somehow better than staying and seeing what delights you have to offer. I thought that since an airplane ticket to get me overseas costs as much as one to Vancouver, I should go overseas . . . because it was somehow better.

I was wrong. Having hosted the show for five years now, I have traversed every one of Canada's provinces and one of the territories (I'll visit soon, Nunavut and Northwest Territories!), a gift for which I am always grateful. After all, how many other guys are able to earn their living while travelling from coast to coast to coast?

And yes, the physical beauty of the country is simply mind-boggling. From the beaches of Atlantic Canada to the majestic sweep of the Prairies, from the Rockies to the bustling pulse of Vancouver, there's a lifetime of sights to see. I've started checking some off my bucket list, but there are plenty more to go.

Then there's the food! Yes, we are a young country, but with youth comes innovation. Over the past half-decade, I have feasted on enough dishes to keep any human smiling for a lifetime. Asian fusion, Rocky Mountain regional, spicy, cheesy, large, small—I've done it all. And the *burgers!* Massive or petite, meaty or seafoody (pretty sure I made that word up!), there's a burger for every culinary whim you could ever imagine. And when it comes to poutine, well, nobody on earth holds a candle to us.

For all the physical beauty and culinary delights that Canada has to offer, the one thing that has resonated with me the most has been the people. No, I don't think we're all cut from angelic cloth, but I can tell you from first-hand experience that we are a nation of giving, thoughtful, generous, and well-intentioned folks. Can we do better? Of course we can. But recognizing that is what makes us uniquely Maple Leaf.

Please accept my humble apology, dear Canada. You might only be home, but you're a pretty freakin' amazing one, indeed.

WESTERN
CANADA

BURNABY, BC, AND SURROUNDING AREA

Fraser Park Restaurant

Est. 1996
4663 Byrne Rd., #103
Burnaby, BC V5J 3H6
(604) 433-7605
www.fraserparkrestaurant.com

. . . .

It's worth the drive to the Middle of Nowhere, say devotees of this irrepressibly down-to-earth restaurant. Chef and owner Anton Heggen is a master sausage maker, a skill he learned from his mother. After honing his meat-carving skills in Berlin, Germany, Anton and his wife, Sylvia, opened Fraser Park in 1996. Featuring meats made daily on-site, popular items include the German Breakfast, the German Deluxe, and the Beef Dip Plate—all belly-warming experiences. Try to fight the urge to yodel.

Hilltop Diner

Est. 1942
23904 Fraser Highway
Langley, BC V2Z 2K8
(604) 514-9424

. . . .

Old-school diners usually elicit images of homemade desserts, hefty portions, and a fun-loving family behind it all. That's what you get at the Hilltop. Whether it's the gravy-drenched open meatloaf sandwich, the creamy flapper pie, or the loving banter between owners (sisters Sandie Parley and Andrea Zaiser) and their children (head chef Kris and second cook Jami), the Hilltop is a classic in every sense of the word. It's even been a movie set!

LOCAL GEM

Tour Simon Fraser University, Burnaby Campus

Whether you're preparing for university or not, there's nothing quite like touring a university campus. Nestled on the top of Burnaby Mountain, Simon Fraser University is one of BC's best and brightest. Visit the campus and see what it's like for more than 30,000 students who walk the same paths every year. Sign up for a student-led tour or walk the sprawling grounds on your own to check out the unique architecture and beautiful scenery that the university has to offer. 8888 University Dr., Burnaby, BC, V5A 1S6. www.sfu.ca/students/tour/book-a -burnaby-tour.html.

The Hilltop Diner's original sign

Flapper Pie (Hilltop Diner)

Simon Fraser University

Beef Dip Plate (Fraser Park Restaurant)

CALGARY, AB

Beer Revolution
Est. 2011
1080 8th St. SW
Calgary, AB T2R 0J3
(403) 264-2739
www.beerrevolution.ca

· · · · · · · · · · · · · · · ·

Pizza and beer are like John Catucci and plaid: great on their own and even better together. And with pizza this inventive—we're talking spring rolls stuffed with pepperoni or an entire Alberta steak on a pizza—Calgary's Beer Revolution is all about delicious surprises. In this laid-back dining room, Calgarians take a break from the daily grind. Every day's a pizza party around here, and chef Mark Jekschtat's Blazing Saddle Pizza is king of the rodeo.

Big Fish
Est. 2004
1112 Edmonton Trail NE
Calgary, AB T2E 3K4
(403) 277-3403
www.big-fish.ca

· · · · · · · · · · · ·

Owned by Dwayne Ennest and his wife, Alberta, Big Fish is converting beef-loving Cowtown residents into seafood aficionados. Try the Lamb and Lobster Burger, Dwayne's addition to the annals of surf-and-turf-dom, or order Big Fish's Bucket of Peel and Eat Shrimp, a communal, get-yer-hands-dirty dish. Other favourites include the Lobster Poutine and the Steelhead Trout Burger with homemade blueberry barbecue sauce. If you're at the Stampede craving the taste of the sea, Big Fish is your place.

Big T's BBQ & Smokehouse
Est. 2004
2138 Crowchild Trail NW
Calgary, AB T2M 3Y7
(403) 284-5959
www.bigtsbbq.com

· · · · · · · · · · · ·

If you're opening a Calgary meatery, you better know what you're doing. Luckily, chef Nikki Bond at Big T's is a tried-and-true student of authentic Southern barbecue. This place serves it up large. Take the signature Elvis Platter, a dish so huge you need a chuckwagon to haul it. From the Gutbuster sandwich to the meatloaf, meat—and meat smoking—defines Big T's. Signs you've been here? The size of your gut and the grin on your face.

Boogie's Burgers

Est. 1969
908A Edmonton Trail NE
Calgary, AB T2E 3K1
(403) 230-7070
www.boogiesburgers.com
. . . .

At Boogie's Burgers, Fat Elvis is king . . . and also a milkshake big enough to be a meal (nothing says thirst-quenching quite like bacon, its not-so-secret ingredient). Founded in 1969 by Gus Pieters, owner of Calgary's famous Peters' Drive-In, along with his brother and their friend, Boogie, the restaurant was later sold and turned into a family stop. In 2008, Noel Sweetland and Kipp Teghtmeyer returned Boogie's to its roots. Classic '80s decor and sloppy creations, like the pizza-flavoured Keith's Burger, make Boogie's a *You Gotta Eat Here!* Fan Favourite.

Bookers BBQ Grill and Crab Shack

Est. 1998
316 3rd St. SE, #10
Calgary, AB T2G 2S4
(403) 264-6419
www.bookersbbq.com
. . . .

Bookers BBQ Grill and Crab Shack brings Southern flavours to the Great White North. From Memphis barbecue spice rubs to Kansas City–style barbecue sauce, chef Myles Learning has scoured the South for its best recipes. Every Sunday and Monday, Calgarians head to Bookers for their all-you-can-eat ribs and crab—they sell around 600 pounds of crab and 65 to 85 racks of ribs a night! Full-bellied customers leave Bookers licking their fingers and loosening their belts.

The Bro'kin Yolk

Est. 2015
12580 Symons Valley Rd. NW, #130
Calgary, AB T3P 0A3
(587) 317-5743
www.brokinyolk.ca
. . . .

It's golden yolks and hearts at the Bro'kin Yolk, a Calgary breakfast hot spot. Brothers Jeff and Gil Carlos run this family-friendly joint serving up crispy Belgian waffles, bennies, and breakfast bowls in a sixty-seat gingham-clad space. Jeff uses almost 4,000 eggs,

Chef Myles Learning (Bookers BBQ Grill and Crab Shack)

Old-Fashioned Montreal Smoked Meat Sandwich (Grumans Delicatessen)

Chef Joshua Hobin
(The Fine Diner Bistro)

Grumans Delicatessen

750 pounds of potatoes, and over 130 pounds of bacon every week! Jeff and Gil also support the local community, donating the proceeds from their water sales to KidSport Calgary.

Diner Deluxe
Est. 2001
804 Edmonton Trail NE
Calgary, AB T2E 3J6
(403) 276-5499
www.dinerdeluxe.com

. . . .

At Diner Deluxe, the lines start early and last all day, especially during its famous brunch—but don't let that stop you. Add the Deluxe's Maple Fried Oatmeal, Meatloaf Hash, and French Toast to the list of Good Things That Come to Those Who Wait. Always looking for new twists on old standbys, chef James Waters creates culinary masterpieces. So put on your parka. Foodie nirvana is waiting . . . if you're willing to wait, too.

The Fine Diner Bistro
Est. 2012
1420 9th Ave. SE, #4
Calgary, AB T2G 0T5
(403) 234-8885
www.finedinerbistro.ca

. . . .

In Inglewood, Calgary's oldest neighbourhood, the Fine Diner is classic diner food for the 21st century. Chef Joshua Hobin and his team are serving up surf and turf mac 'n' cheese, "lambtastic" lamb shank, and pomegranate chicken. With bright, crisp colours, the restaurant provides an atmosphere that's as fresh and fun as the food. When it comes to diner style, the Fine Diner is throwing away the old-school philosophy.

Grumans Delicatessen
Est. 2012
230 11th Ave. SE
Calgary, AB T2G 0X8
(403) 261-9003
www.grumans.ca

. . . .

Think you need to go to Montreal to find great Jewish deli food? Think again! Grumans Delicatessen brings smoked meat and plenty of hearty noshing to the good, lucky people of Calgary. It's the only place of its kind in town.

Owner Peter's secret weapon is his mom, Bubby, whose recipes are sprinkled throughout the menu. She says, "People are always looking for the perfect recipe for happiness. I always look in two places, my heart and my oven." Deli-cious!

Holy Grill

Est. 2003
827 10th Ave. SW
Calgary, AB T2R 0A9
(403) 261-9759
www.holygrill.ca
· · · · · · · · · · · ·

Early patrons were confused by Holy Grill's unique name (is it a restaurant or house of worship?), but word soon spread about its heavenly dishes. Run by Nick, John, and Andrew Yee and known for its breakfasts and lunches, Holy Grill is a favourite. John loves the South Beach Benny with Bacon and truly mind-blowing Smash Browns, and the Yee brothers' famous panini. Don't forget the homemade beetroot chips.

Jelly Modern Doughnuts

Est. 2011
1414 8th St. SW, #100
Calgary, AB T2R 1J6
(403) 453-2053
www.jellymoderndoughnuts.com
· ·

We Canucks are tried-and-true doughnut eaters. Inspired by mom-and-pop shops, sisters Rita and Roseanne Tripathy created Jelly Modern, recruiting pastry chef Grayson Sherman to transform this everyday food into edible art. With more than twenty-five varieties of cake and raised doughnuts, from a hand-fried apple fritter to whoopie pie, Jelly Modern is reinventing the wheel. But if there's only one doughnut that demonstrates love of this country, it's the maple bacon. It's like Canada in your mouth . . . only without the rocks and wood.

Naina's Kitchen

Est. 2010
121 17th Ave. SE
Calgary, AB T2G 1H3
(403) 263-6355
www.nainaskitchen.com
· · · · · · · · · · · · · · · · ·

Whether you call her Naina, Nonna, or Nana, nothing's better than eating in grandma's kitchen. She never lets you go hungry. At Naina's Kitchen you can eat whatever you want, as much as you want. So go ahead! Order chef Erin Mueller's Breakfast Poutine or Naina's favourite stuffed burger, there's no judgment here—just pure happiness. This home away from home has busy business folk loosening their ties, kicking off their heels, and pulling up a chair.

Oak Tree Tavern

Est. 2011
124B 10th St. NW
Calgary, AB T2N 1V3
(403) 270-3347
www.oaktreetavern.ca
· · · · · · · · · · · · · · · · ·

Oak Tree Tavern is a buzzing Kensington neighbourhood hot spot where chef Nicole Dekuysscher serves up pub hits with twists that keep Calgarians coming back. From spicy coconut curry fries to carrot-and-yam hummus, beef and Guinness stew, and super Sloppy Joes, there's something for everyone at Oak Tree Tavern. Try the delicious dill pickle soup!

The Palomino Smokehouse
Est. 2005
109 7th Ave. SW
Calgary, AB T2P 0W5
(403) 532-1911
www.thepalomino.ca
. . . .

The Palomino Smokehouse serves up authentic smoked barbecue with a side-order of honky-tonk ambience. You'll find hearty helpings of Alberta beef brisket, Kansas City pork ribs, and bacon-wrapped corn cobs. The Palomino brings a road trip's worth of barbecue to your table! With a dining room and patio that can seat 250 total, the Palomino needs a smoker that can keep up. Theirs can hold up to 700 pounds of meat. It runs at full capacity during the Stampede. *Yeehaw!*

Pfanntastic Pannenkoek Haus
Est. 1997
2439 54th Ave. SW
Calgary, AB T3E 1M4
(403) 243-7757
www.dutchpancakes.ca
. . . .

In a city that prides itself on pancakes, there's an unassuming restaurant bucking the trend. Fluffy flapjacks are strictly verboten at the Pfanntastic Pannenkoek Haus, home to the giant crêpes the Dutch have been eating for centuries. In the Netherlands, a pannenkoek is eaten for lunch or dinner. Owner Denice Greenwald and pannenkoek handyman Joe Payne serve them all day, adding flair to the traditional undertaking and offering eighty kinds, including the Kaneel Rol (cinnamon roll) and Steak Met Smeerkaas (Philly cheesesteak). Take that, Stampede breakfast!

Pig & Duke

Est. 2012
503 4th Ave. SW
Calgary, AB T2P 0J7
(403) 452-0539
www.pigandduke.ca

. . . .

When you're looking to dine on swine in the heart of Cowtown, come on down to Pig & Duke! Chef Evan Robertson left the fine dining scene to try his hand at comfort food. Try the kielbasa, the meatloaf, or the Canuck Burger. BC natives Evan and owner Stephen Lowden admit it's a little gutsy naming a burger after their hometown hockey team in Flames territory. They pretend the Canuck Burger is named because of the Canadian back bacon, especially if there's a game on.

Tubby Dog

Est. 2005
1022 17th Ave. SW
Calgary, AB T2T 0A5
(403) 244-0694
www.tubbydog.com

. . . .

Art student and bartender Jon Truch wasn't sure how to kick-start business on slow weeknights. Then someone gave him a hot dog rotisserie. Light bulb! Soon wieners drew in more people than drinks did, and Jon knew that his future was in the art of the dog. Tubby Dog was born. Now the restaurant is a Calgary phenomenon. Jon sculpts meat-and-bread creations that Michelangelo himself would be proud of. Try the Sumo, the A-bomb, or Sherm's Ultimate Gripper, dogs challenging both to describe and to eat.

UNA Pizza & Wine

Est. 2010
618 17th Ave. SW
Calgary, AB T2S 0B4
(403) 453-1183
www.unapizzeria.com/calgary

. . . .

The moment you arrive at UNA, you're immediately part of the family. Here the kitchen is the focal point, the servers and cooks are friends, and you'll have a great chat with other customers about the tender veal and pork meatballs. Another UNA specialty, pizzas here are constantly on the move, rotating between the top and bottom of the oven and to different temperature spots on each level. It's fast, it's hot, and just like comedy, it's all about timing.

Oak Tree Tavern

Canuck Burger (Pig & Duke)

Sloppy Joes (Oak Tree Tavern)

Sliced Alberta Beef Brisket
(The Palomino Smokehouse)

UNA Pizza & Wine

LOCAL GEMS

Extreme Air Park

Visit Canada's largest trampoline park for a fun adventure for the whole family. With over 42,000 square feet of interlocking trampolines that features two jump courts, three 3D dodgeball courts, trampoline basketball, an eight-lane foam dive pit, and much more, you're sure to have a fun family adventure. Make a reservation online, or simply drop in and you'll be given full access to all that Extreme Air Park has to offer. 1411 33rd St. NE, Calgary, AB, T2A 5P1. www.calgary .extremeairpark.com.

Vin Gogh

If you're feeling a little artistic, check out this unique "paint and sip" clubhouse that lets you reimagine classic works of art with your own paintbrush, all while sipping on a nice glass of wine. All you have to do to sign up is choose a night or your favourite painting, then enjoy the experience. You'll be guided by an artist who can help you perfect your re-creation, but you're welcome to craft your own spin on the classics as well. #118–7004 MacLeod Trail SE, Calgary, AB, T2H 0L3. www.vingogh.ca.

Year-Round Horseback Riding

If you're looking for adventure and want to get back to nature, take in one of Alberta's most famous activities: horseback riding. Offered year-round (weather permitting) from a variety of different ranches and tour operators, it lets you see Alberta the way it's meant to be seen: from on top of a horse. There are six major locations in operation within close proximity to Calgary, so you can choose how you want to experience horseback riding. Whether it's a day trip, classes, or a week-long adventure, there are always plenty of options at your fingertips. www.visitcalgary.com/things-to-do/sports-recreation/horseback-riding.

Day Trip to Drumheller

Take a day trip to Drumheller, the dinosaur capital of the world. Located an hour and a half northeast of Calgary, Drumheller has a little something for everyone. With a mix of dinosaur-themed museums and gift shops and hikes through the historic Badlands, it's definitely worth the drive. Take a hike in Horseshoe Canyon or visit the Hoodoo Trails to get your fill of the beautiful Alberta landscape. Or visit the Royal Tyrell Museum and the world's largest dinosaur attraction to unleash your inner paleontologist. www.traveldrumheller.com.

What's with The Fork?
A *You Gotta Go Here!* Choose Your Own Adventure

As much as I hate to admit it, The Fork is likely a more important part of *You Gotta Eat Here!* than I am. I mean, everyone asks me about The Fork. In fact, I wouldn't be surprised if The Fork ends up hosting the show and I get the can. But before I walk off into the sunset, you should know the story of The Fork and how it came to play such an important role in my life. But be warned, it may not be quite as romantic as you've imagined. Aww, what the heck. I'll give you a couple options, depending on which tale you like telling yourself (ain't I sweet?):

- If you want the real story of The Fork, go to paragraph 3.
- If you want to continue living in Fairyland, go to paragraph 2.

When I was but a boy, my dear *nonna* took me aside during one of our Christmas Eve family gatherings. The air was thick with the smell of her delicious cooking. I had never seen her look so angelic in her apron. "My little bambino," she cooed as she propped me on her spacious lap, "I see food in your future. I'm not sure how or why, but I know you will need this." With that, she reached inside her apron and pulled out The Fork. It gleamed in the light of the Christmas tree. My little jaw dropped. Somewhere in the distance I could hear angels singing. "Look," she said, turning it over to reveal an engraving underneath. "It belonged to the Pope. Take it with you on your travels and never forget that food can be a holy experience." I tucked The Fork in my back pocket and have cherished it ever since.

Okay, so I don't *really* carry the same fork from city to city, restaurant to restaurant. It just so happens that while shooting one of the earliest episodes of *You Gotta Eat Here!*, I needed a place to stash a fork that someone had just handed me. I slipped it in my back pocket without even thinking twice.

When it came time to sample the food in front of me, the chef offered me a different fork. That's when my steel-trap memory kicked in and I pulled the one out of my pocket. The chef laughed. I laughed. Everyone else giggled. A moment was born.

Since then, stashing cutlery in my back pocket has become tradition—even if it's not always a fork. Sometimes it's chopsticks, occasionally a dessert spoon. But never, ever a fillet knife. And no, I've *never* inadvertently sat down on a fork, either. (C'mon, I'm a *professional*, people!)

If you're one of those generous types who can't control your desire to gift me a fork (you'd be surprised how many I've gotten over the years), remember that what I *really* want is a telescopic one so I can steal a fry from the guy beside me when he's looking at his phone.

It's not telescopic and doesn't seem to have been used by the Pope, but this bad-boy served me well for at least . . . um . . . one episode.

CANMORE AND BANFF, AB

The Bear Street Tavern
Est. 2006
211 Bear St.
Banff, AB T1L 1A1
(403) 762-2021
www.bearstreettavern.ca
. . . .

Originally a general store that served fresh cheeses and deli meats, the Bear Street Tavern celebrates the humble beginning that still underpins its philosophy— great, fresh, simple sandwiches, pizzas, and classics that everyone enjoys.

Chef Kirk Thompson slow cooks bison and fries up Canadian back bacon in a casual, rustic atmosphere. Come straight in from downhill skiing or stop by for lunch while you're backpacking. This is good old-fashioned Rocky Mountain eating—a delicious tribute to the Great White North!

The Crazyweed Kitchen
Est. 1997
1600 Railway Ave.
Canmore, AB T1W 1P6
(403) 609-2530
www.crazyweed.ca
. . . .

You wouldn't think you'd find fusion comfort food up in the mountains, but the Crazyweed Kitchen is Canmore's hot spot for some *crazy* twists on the food you know and love. Think Vietnamese meatballs and Singapore-style curry, dishes that are stopping the residents of this Rocky Mountain town in their tracks! Owner Jan Hrabec named her restaurant while reading a Rocky Mountain flower guide. When she found the "crazyweed" flower, the name stuck!

LOCAL GEMS

Elevation Place

If you want to swim laps or splash about, work up a sweat or climb the day away, Elevation Place is where it's at in Canmore. It features an eight-lane lap pool, a beach-style leisure pool, and a 25-person hot tub as well as a 40-foot climbing wall with auto-belay systems, a bouldering area, and over 100 different climbing routes. There is also a fully equipped weight room, and fitness studios are available for use. Elevation Place offers day passes for individuals and families. 700 Railway Ave., Canmore, AB, T1W 1P4. www.canmore.ca/recreation-facility /elevation-place.

Whyte Museum of the Canadian Rockies

Discover the heritage of the Rocky Mountains at the Whyte Museum of the Canadian Rockies. The vast collection of artwork spans from the early 1800s to the present day, while the heritage collection contains artifacts from early Aboriginals, immigrants, mountaineers, and more. The museum even features public archives with photos, books, newspaper articles, commercial films, and sound recordings spanning the history of Banff, Alberta, and the Rocky Mountains. 111 Bear St., Banff, AB, T1L 1A3. www.whyte.org.

Whyte Museum of the Canadian Rockies

EDMONTON, AB

Battista's Calzone Co.
Est. 2010
11745 84th St. NW
Edmonton, AB T5B 3C2
(780) 758-1808
www.battistacalzone.com
. . . .

It's calzones or bust at Battista's Calzone Co., home of perfect pockets of dough, sauce, and cheese. From the New York Mama, overflowing with homemade meatloaf, to the Buon Giorno, with spicy pancetta and eggs, chef Battista Vecchio's food is fresh, interesting, and filled with love. In fact, the food is so good that one impressed customer decided to quit her job and become Battista's current partner—now that's an endorsement! Battista's is not to be missed.

The Dish Bistro and the Runaway Spoon
Est. 1996
12417 Stony Plain Rd. NW
Edmonton, AB T5N 3N3
(780) 488-6641
www.thedishandspoon.com
. . . .

In 1996, Carole Amerongen plunged fork-first into her dream of owning a restaurant. Accomplished musician and chef Michael Verchomin joined the fold a few years later, and they've been making beautiful music ever since. The occasional jazz riff ringing out of the kitchen is just Michael's way of celebrating *his* two great loves. Every item on the menu hits the high notes, from the Cherry Short Ribs to the Deep Dish Sweet Potato Shepherd's Pie. The symphony of flavours leaves all customers singing the Dish's praises.

Highlevel Diner
Est. 1982
10912 88th Ave. NW
Edmonton, AB T6G 0Z1
(780) 433-0993
www.highleveldiner.com
. . . .

The year was 1982: *Thriller* was released, the Great One wore Oilers orange and blue, and the Highlevel Diner was born. Three decades later, the Highlevel's world-class cinnamon buns taste as good as ever. Owner Kim Franklin and chefs Debbie Parker and Adam Stoyko know that homemade food never goes out of style. Favourites include the Spinach Pie, Middle Eastern Platter, and Ural Burger, a recipe carried by an original owner's grandmother across the Ural Mountains into Bulgaria. The Highlevel's a timeless classic.

Louisiana Purchase
Est. 1989
10320 111th St. NW
Edmonton, AB T5K 1M9
(780) 420-6779
www.louisianapurchase.ca
· · · · · · · · · · · · · · · · · · ·

There's fine Southern cookin' being served up 3700 kilometres from the bayou! The Louisiana Purchase is a Creole cuisine—lover's delight, feeding locals, tourists, and rock legends for over two decades. Since original owner Dennis Vermette retired in 2011, the Halabi family has respected the restaurant's storied past while putting their own thumbprint on it. Try the Alligator Kebabs or an old-time favourite, the Satisfaction Plate, so named when the Rolling Stones raved about it. The Louisiana Purchase

brims with fun, flavour, and happy customers.

MEAT
Est. 2014
8216 104th St. NW
Edmonton, AB T6E 4E6
(587) 520-6338
www.meatfordinner.com
· · · · · · · · · · · · · · · · · · ·

Bourbon, brisket, and beer is what it's all about at MEAT, an Edmonton barbecue joint serving Texas-style smoked meat by the pound. Chef Nathan McLaughlin adds some weight to barbecue with delicious sides like mac 'n' cheese and baked beans that you can mix and match to your heart's delight. Choose from one of four house-made barbecue sauces. Are you in the mood for Spicy, Bourbon, Cherry, or Mustard? What about a mixture of a few? Be saucy and choose your own adventure!

29

Rostizado

Est. 2014
10359 104th St., #102
Edmonton, AB T5J 1B9
(706) 761-0911
www.rostizado.com

....

Take your taste buds on a trip to sunny Mexico at Rostizado, a restaurant in the heart of Edmonton serving some killer street food from south of the border. Laid back and unpretentious, like your coolest friend's apartment, Rostizado is the perfect place to hang out with friends and eat rotisserie chicken and pork done in a traditional blend of Mexican spices. Chef and owner Daniel Braun loves warming Edmontonians with Mexican cooking techniques. *Adios*, donuts *hola*, churros!

Sloppy Hoggs Roed Hus

Est. 2012
9563A 118th Ave.
Edmonton, AB T5G 0N9
(780) 477-2408
www.sloppyhoggsbbq.com

....

The wild worlds of Southern barbecue and extreme burgers collide at Sloppy Hoggs Roed Hus in Edmonton. Wrangling these outrageous burgers will require some chest beating and a lot of conviction. Check out the Sloppy Hog, a pork lover's dream burger: Chef Brenda Dutton combines her signature pork patty and smoked pork butt . . . then things really start to get sloppy! And don't forget My Ridiculous Fat Ass burger, loaded with smoked beef brisket. Cow skulls and cattle-herding paraphernalia fill the space, keeping the Wild West atmosphere alive. Meatatarians unite!

Soda Jerks Burgers & Bottles

Est. 2011
16616 95th St.
Edmonton, AB T5Z 3L2
(587) 521-9311
www.sodajerks.net

....

Imagine if a fourteen-year-old kid opened the burger joint of his dreams. Chances are it would look just like Soda Jerks in Edmonton: crazy, delicious, a place where toppings rule. Nachos on a burger?

Neon Sign Museum

Macho Nacho Burger
(Soda Jerks Burgers & Bottles)

Baklava (Sofra)

Alligator Kebab (Louisiana Purchase)

What about a PB&J waffle burger? Or consider a Baba Burger topped with mouth-watering perogies! Owner Lance Popke wanted his customers to indulge in their favourite childhood snacks in a fun new way. For an adult upgrade, try the Big Kid Floats (vodka-based shakes). Wash that burger down!

Sofra
Est. 2006
10345 106th St. NW
Edmonton, AB T5J 0J2
(780) 423-3044
· · · · · · · · · · ·

Sofra was John's maiden voyage to the spicy world of Turkish cuisine and a memorable one thanks to chef Yuksel Gultekin and his wife, Chandra. Try the Adana Kebab, a belly-warming meal cooked and prepared on a sword! Don't miss the canoe-shaped Ispanakli Pideler (Turkish pizza), one of the twenty-five best things to eat in Edmonton according to a local magazine. Break out of your shell, Canada! Sofra's ridiculously tasty creations are world class.

Sugarbowl
Est. 1942
10922 88th Ave.
Edmonton, AB T6G 0Z1
(780) 433-8369
www.thesugarbowl.org
· · · · · · · · · · · · · · · ·

Someone call Charles Darwin, because the Sugarbowl's been evolving since it first opened in 1942. Now among Edmonton's premier comfort restaurants, it's home to Abel Shiferaw's cinnamon buns, one of the best reasons to visit Edmonton. These treats are so popular that loving parents often ship them to their kids at university. From the chicken and waffles to the lamb and goat cheese burger, every item on the menu seems to have that special combination of inventiveness, size, warmth, and love.

Tres Carnales Taquería
Est. 2011
10119 100A St. NW
Edmonton, AB T5J 0R5
(780) 429-0911
www.trescarnales.com
· · · · · · · · · · · · · · · · ·

The brainchild of three amigos, Edgar Gutierrez, Daniel Braun, and Chris Sills, Tres Carnales has had a huge impact on the Edmonton food scene, wowing its customers with authenticity. They make eight different fillings for tacos, quesadillas, or tortas. The one that set John's heart a-skippin' was the Al Pastor. Vibrant, lively, and welcoming, with an open kitchen and Mexican hip hop playing in the background, Tres Carnales is a taste of Mexico in the gateway to the North.

Urban Diner
Est. 2004
12427 102nd Ave. NW
Edmonton, AB T5N 0M2
(780) 488-7274
www.urbandiner.com

. . . .

When a classically trained Dutch chef moves to Edmonton and can't find his favourite foods, he can either move back to Holland or do something about it. For Cyrilles Koppert and partner Lisa Dungale, the choice was clear. At the Urban Diner's two locations, people brave ungodly temperatures to line up for a taste of Cyrilles's recipes. John's favourite? Traditional poffertjes, which shrink everything you love about pancakes into a tiny package—one of many delicious dishes from this Dutch chef on a mission.

LOCAL GEMS

Jurassic Forest

Experience millions of years of history in Jurassic Forest, a unique location featuring realistic, life-sized dinosaur models, all just a 45-minute drive north from Edmonton. This prehistoric site uses the natural beauty of the surrounding old-growth forest to offer visitors a spectacular journey through the Jurassic era. Set off on your guided journey to see the dinosaurs in action and take in the local flora and fauna from over 250 million years ago. #2-23210 Township Road 564, Gibbons, AB, T0A 1N0. www.jurassicforest.com.

Neon Sign Museum

The Neon Sign Museum is an outdoor display of Edmonton's bright and buzzing past. Best enjoyed at night, this museum features twelve neon signs from throughout Edmonton's history. Signs on display include classic logos and advertisements for bakeries, auto shops, theatres, arcades, and more. Each commercial sign was chosen to represent the city's unique vintage signage during the eras of the past. 104th St. NW, Edmonton, AB, T5J 0K7. www.edmonton.ca/city_government/edmonton_archives/neon-sign-museum.aspx.

GIBSONS, BC

Smitty's Oyster House
Est. 2007
643 School Road Wharf
Lower Gibsons, BC V0N 1V0
(604) 886-4665
www.smittysoysterhouse.com

. . . .

Talk about "fresh" food: At Stafford Lumley and Shawn Divers's restaurant, you can literally watch the menu being loaded off the docked trawlers. Here you'll find the seafood joint that all others want to be when they grow up. With an unmatched rustic feel, Smitty's is the perfect setting for chef Conor Lowe's marvellous Oyster Po' Boy and Halibut Fritters. While it boasts the comfort and relaxed attitude that goes with small-town living, its taste and selection is all big city.

LOCAL GEM
Sunshine Coast Olive Oil Co.

A family-owned operation, the Sunshine Coast Olive Oil Company was born after a trip to Italy opened the eyes of owners Matt Lunny and Fiona Pinnell to the health benefits of olive oil. Not only do they offer a wide assortment of some of the best oils, seasonings, and foods from around the world, but they also have free tastings and the occasional cooking class. The shop is part of the Ultra Premium program, meaning all its products must meet or exceed rigorous standards before being sold to customers. 287 Gower Point Rd., #305, Gibsons, BC, V0N 1V0. www.sunshinecoastoliveoil.com.

JASPER, AB

Downstream Lounge
Est. 2008
620 Connaught Dr.
Jasper, AB T0E 1E0
(780) 852-9449
www.downstreamjasper.ca

. . . .

Sotirios "Soto" Korogonas cooks up hearty and delicious wild game in the gorgeous Rocky Mountains. In Greek, *sotirios* means "salvation." Enjoy just one of his dishes and—*holy moly!*—you'll understand why the name fits. Serving a variety of locally butchered meats, like juicy fall-off-the-bone bison short ribs or tender elk steaks with Saskatoon berry reduction, the Downstream Lounge is a must-stop destination.

LOCAL GEM
Jasper Motorcycle Tours

Hop in the sidecar and get your camera ready for a rockin' good time. Jasper Motorcycle Tours allows you to live your Harley Davidson dream with the aid of skilled motorcyclists leading the way. Get dressed in leather from head to foot and ride through Jasper National Park and the Canadian Rockies. Explore one of Canada's most beautiful parks in style and go on a grand adventure you won't soon forget. 610 Patricia St., Jasper, AB, T0E 1E0. www.jaspermotorcycletours .com/sidecar.html.

KAMLOOPS, BC

Fiesta Mexicana
Est. 2011
793 Notre Dame Dr.
Kamloops, BC V2C 5N8
(250) 374-3960
www.fiestamexicana.ca

. . . .

Want to visit Mexico without leaving
Kamloops? You can, thanks to Rodd
Cruikshank and Liz Lujan, owners
of Fiesta Mexicana, a light, friendly,
and fun place to enjoy authentic
south of the border cuisine. Originally from Guadalajara, chef Alberto
"Beto" Vazquez is the restaurant's
lifeblood, putting his passion into
every dish he creates, especially his
world-class Enchiladas Poblanas.
Make sure you save room for deep-
fried ice cream. It's a classic way to
finish off a visit to Mexico.

LOCAL GEM
Go Geocaching

Geocaching is a popular activity
around the world and an interesting
way to get out and about exploring
new areas. Try your hand at it in
Kamloops, where multiple locations
are just waiting to be discovered.
This treasure hunt/exchange game
is a great way to get exercise, learn
valuable navigation skills, and just
enjoy yourself. Fun for all ages, easy
to get started, and completely free,
geocaching is an adventure waiting to
happen. www.tourismkamloops.com/
geocaching-in-kamloops-bc.

KELOWNA, BC, AND SURROUNDING AREA

The Jammery
Est. 2000
8038 Highway 97 N
Kelowna, BC V4V 1T3
(250) 766-1139
www.jammery.com
. . . .

The Jammery is Kelowna's best spot to grab all-day breakfast. Their zany take on morning meal favourites—like breakfast bacon cheeseburger, Spanish-inspired chorizo toss, and all-you-can-eat waffles—are sure to pump up the jam in your day. And it wouldn't be the Jammery without some delicious homemade preserves. They make almost forty different kinds on-site so don't forget to grab a jar on your way out! The Jammery has a little something for everyone.

Kekuli Café
Est. 2009
3041 Louie Dr., #505
Westbank, BC V4T 3E2
(250) 768-3555
www.kekulicafe.com
. . . .

Bannock, long a staple for First Nations Canadians, is the cornerstone of the Kekuli's menu. Owner, self-taught chef, and proud member of the Nooaitch First Nation Sharon Bond ushers the traditional dish into the 21st century. As the Kekuli boasts to its guests, "Don't panic . . . We have bannock!" Faves include the Breakfast Bannock and the Bannock Burger. Fried or baked, sweet or savoury, bannock satisfies all your doughy needs.

Chuckwagon Cafe & Cattle Co.
Est. 1973
105 Sunset Blvd.
Turner Valley, AB T0L 2A0
(403) 933-0003
www.chuckwagoncafe.ca
. . . .

Here in cowboy country, classic Western dishes are the food *du jour*, and owner Terry Myhre raises the Chuckwagon's beef himself! Burgers and steaks are king, no matter what time of day. Two faves are the Flat Iron Steak Benedict and Mushroom and Swiss Burger. There are items on the menu that don't include beef—such as the chicken club or the grilled cheese sandwiches. But not the soup. It's a beef barley that Terry's been perfecting for years!

Two Guys and a Pizza Place
Est. 2002
316 11th St. S
Lethbridge, AB T1J 2N8
(403) 331-2222
www.twoguyspizza.ca
. . . .

Two Guys and a Pizza Place turns your favourite gourmet sand-wiches into amazing pizzas. Whether you're craving pulled pork or an Italian Club, Two Guys has a pie for you. Owner Cory Medd has been crowned Canada's best pizza chef twice by *Canadian Pizza* magazine, and he competes every year at the International Pizza Challenge in Vegas, where he's made it to the finals twice. Sounds like a winning recipe!

LOCAL GEM

Day Trip to Vulcan

Take a trip to Alberta's final frontier: Vulcan, the *Star Trek* capital of Canada. The town shares the name of the home planet of one of science fiction's most iconic characters, Spock, and offers visitors an experience unlike any other. With themed adventures, businesses, and locations spread across the town, Vulcan is sure to please any *Star Trek* fan. Don't forget to take a trip to the Vulcan Tourism and Trek Station, which features a gift shop containing every colour of Starfleet shirt and even a replica captain's chair. www.townofvulcan.ca.

Chuckwagon Cafe & Cattle Co.

Vulcan, AB

Classic Pulled Pork Pizza (Two Guys and a Pizza Place)

MOOSE JAW, SK

Deja Vu Cafe
Est. 2007
16 High St. E
Moose Jaw, SK S6H 0B7
(306) 692-6066
www.dejavucafe.ca

. . . .

Owner Brandon Richardson has one approach when it comes to food: Let's deep-fry this sucker! And judging by the devout following, fellow Moose Javians share his philosophy. Chicken is the highlight of a menu that never takes itself too seriously. One hundred exotic sauce creations also come home to roost, adding great variety. Choosing is hard when it comes to the eighty flavours of milkshakes, too. How are you supposed to pick? You'll be fried just thinking about it.

LOCAL GEM
Tunnels of Moose Jaw

Take a trip through the underground and discover Moose Jaw's local history. The tunnels of Moose Jaw let attendees enjoy an interactive experience told through stories and re-enactments. With two tour options (Passage to Fortune and The Chicago Connection), you'll get to become a character and experience a part of Moose Jaw's colourful history. The Passage to Fortune puts you in the shoes of early Chinese immigrants, while The Chicago Connection explores Moose Jaw's connection to Al Capone by turning you into a bootlegger during the era of his reign.
18 Main St. N., Moose Jaw, SK, S6H 3J6. www.tunnelsofmoosejaw.com.

You Gotta Have It!
John's Travel Bag
Must-Haves

Life on the road can be fun, but it has its challenges, too. In the beginning (when I was just a young'un trying to make my way in the food world), I would just throw stuff in a bag willy-nilly and figure it out once I hit the hotel. Do that a few times and you quickly realize all the stuff you forgot . . . and kinda need. Now I'm a much savvier bag-packer. I know exactly what's gotta go in my suitcase to keep me sane while away from home.

#1: My Trusty Jump Rope

What, you thought jump ropes were just for professional boxers and MMA fighters? Well, okay . . . they might be. But you can add this guy into the mix. No, I'm not entering the ring any time soon, but it's still a great way for me to burn off all those burgers and fries, especially when there's no gym at the hotel. I also travel with a couple sets of exercise bands, just in case I decide to change professions.

#2: An Embarrassingly Hefty Makeup Kit

I remember when all my face stuff fit into a manly toiletry bag. Yep, those were the days. But weeks on end standing over a flat-top grill does things to a guy's face, and my bag grew. Now I pack a full-fledged makeup bag—and it doesn't even have any makeup in it! Instead, I carry a vast array of skin creams (to keep my skin young and moist!), toners, and exfoliators. Then there's all the stuff I need to wash all that stuff *off*. Yeah, my wife gave me a little side eye when she first saw it. But I'm manly in other ways, okay?

#3: Entertainment!

Not that my buddies on the crew aren't entertaining—because they are, like, *really* entertaining—but a guy needs his distractions from time to time. My iPad is just the thing for reading books or comics (*love* my comics!) or even playing games. And yes, I did have a weird Candy Crush habit for a while. Like you didn't?

#4: My Nifty New Pillow

Yes, I'm a germ weirdo. But believe it or not, that's not the main reason why I carry my own pillow (though it may have a *little* to do with it). Mostly, it's because I hate hotel pillows. (Why do they put so many damn pillows on hotel beds, anyway?)

#5: Plaid

Confession time: I don't wear plaid at home. But it's become my trademark outfit on the show, so I carry it everywhere I go. *Lots* of it: two of the exact same shirt for each restaurant we visit, just in case I make a mess. And since we can sometimes be gone for weeks at a time, that's a lotta plaid. I actually carry a separate wardrobe bag just for my on-screen shirts. And yes, I get lots of looks from the airport security people.

No, this is not my closet in Toronto! But it's how I roll on the road, which makes for the occasional sideways glance from airport personnel. The blue one is my favourite.

NANAIMO, BC, AND SURROUNDING AREA

Smokin' George's BBQ
Est. 2010
4131 Mostar Rd., #5
Nanaimo, BC V9T 6A6
(250) 585-2258
www.smokingeorgesbbq.com

. . . .

After visiting Smokin' George's, John's suitcase smelled like a smokehouse for days, reminding him of all the mind-blowing meals he had there. Good food and good times play centre stage at George Kulai and Lea Ortner's down-to-earth joint, and all pretense is checked at the door. Whether you try the Loaded Baked Potato with Pulled Pork, the Deep-Fried Dill Pickles, or Mom's Smokin' Pit Beans, you'll see why people get addicted to this place after just one visit.

LOCAL GEM

Wild Play Nanaimo

Open three seasons a year (spring, summer, and fall), Wild Play's Nanaimo location offers a variety of different "elements" to conquer. If you're looking for a quick adrenaline rush, try their loose line leaps, zip-lines, bungee jumps, or giant swings. If you're looking for a more immersive and extreme experience, try an adventure course, which includes elements of the above plus other challenging high-rope obstacles. Classic adventure courses are offered at different experience levels and even include a course designed specifically for children. 35 Nanaimo River Rd., Nanaimo, BC, V9X 1S5. www.wildplay.com/nanaimo.

REGINA, SK

Fresh & Sweet
Est. 2009
2500 Victoria Ave.
Regina, SK S4P 3X2
(306) 751-2233
www.valleygirlscatering.ca/
index.php/menu/freshandsweet

. . . .

Don't let the "sweet" part of Fresh &
Sweet's name fool you. Cook Beata
Thompson is one tough lady! This
roller-derby queen cooks up quirky
breakfast dishes like strawberry
and goat cheese waffles topped
with balsamic dressing. Run
almost exclusively by bold, loud,
and upbeat women, the restaurant
works in a state of controlled chaos.
Diners love that it has the feel of a
fast-food joint with the rambunc-
tious spirit of a roller-derby bout.

LOCAL GEM
Milky Way Ice Cream

Nothing beats the summer heat quite
like a delicious ice-cream cone, and
Regina's Milky Way ice-cream parlour
is the place to go. With what can
only be described as a gargantuan
menu, it's been one of Regina's go-to
spots since 1956 and always draws a
huge crowd. You might not mind the
wait—it'll give you time to choose your
flavour! Whether you go for a classic
cone or try one of their specialties, every item is sure to please. 910 Victoria
Ave., Regina, SK, S4N 0R7. Open sea-
sonally. www.milkywayicecream.com.

SALMON ARM, BC

Shuswap Pie Company
Est. 2008
331A Alexander St. NE
Salmon Arm, BC V1E 4H7
(250) 832-7992
www.shuswappiecompany.ca

. . . .

At the Shuswap Pie Company, founder Mary Jo Beirnes's motto was "put it in a pie." Pork and applesauce? Put it in a pie! Vegetable curry? Put it in a pie! Blueberries and peaches? Put it in a pie! Now headed up by Tovah Shantz, the Shuswap Pie Company loves experimenting with sweet and savoury creations, and locals and tourists alike love eating them. In this fairly small town, they sell a whopping 150 to 200 pies a day— and that's during the *slow* season. In the summer, it's 300 pies. Make sure you grab one!

LOCAL GEM
The Enchanted Forest

Nestled among the trees just off the Trans-Canada Highway is a secret gem for the whole family to enjoy. The Enchanted Forest brings fairy tales to life with over 350 figurines depicting some of the most famous fairy tales, from Snow White to Goldilocks and the Three Bears, Humpty Dumpty to the Wizard of Oz, and so much more. Take the winding path and find yourself at the foot of BC's tallest treehouse or hop in a row boat and paddle around a beaver pond. 7060 Trans-Canada Highway, Revelstoke, BC, V0E 2S0. www.enchantedforestbc.com.

SASKATOON, SK

Bon Temps Café
Est. 2013
223 2nd Ave. S
Saskatoon, SK S7K 1K8
(306) 242-6617
www.bontempscafe.ca

The good times roll at Saskatoon's Bon Temps Café, where they whip up spicy seafood boils and other Creole favourites. We all know that too much merrymaking can mean trouble, though, so the Bon Temps also offers the Peacemaker, an apologetic po' boy sandwich sure to earn anyone's forgiveness and "guaranteed to appease an angry lover or spouse." So bring ya mama'n'em, grab a booth by the jazz-playing skeletons, and party without worries. Every day's Mardi Gras at the Bon Temps Café.

EE Burritos
Est. 2003
705 Central Ave.
Saskatoon, SK S7N 2S4
(306) 343-6264
www.eeburritossaskatoon.com

You can bet your bottom burrito that Salvadoran cuisine is not one of the things Saskatoon is known for—until now. One trip to EE Burritos will convert you to the Central American side of life, thanks to chefs and owners Kathleen Lipinski and Manrique Medrano, who serve up a tamale so big that customers dub it a "lunch box in a banana leaf." Also try Kathleen's papusas. Be one of the eager diners who flock here for a lively Latin American twist on comfort food.

Homestead Ice Cream

Est. 1978
822 Victoria Ave.
Saskatoon, SK S7N 0Z4
(306) 653-5588
www.homesteadicecream.ca

. . . .

Homestead Ice Cream is *the only* place to go in Saskatoon for your summertime ice-cream fix, serving 350 flavours of premium homemade ice cream in sundaes, floats, milkshakes, and splits. Scoop-master Allen Malberg's got every flavour under the sun, from apple pie and brandied peach to peanut dill pickle and chocolate chai. Going through up to eighty eleven-litre buckets of ice cream in a long weekend, Allen satisfies Saskatoon's insatiable ice-cream appetite. Cool as a cone, and then some! Many of the flavours are seasonal, so prepare to make some new discoveries when you visit!

Prairie Harvest Café

Est. 2012
2917 Early Dr.
Saskatoon, SK S7H 3K5
(306) 242-2928
www.prairieharvestcafe.com

. . . .

This homey Saskatoon destination sets the Saskatchewan standard for quirky, scratch-made comfort dishes. Chef Mike McKeown keeps locals coming back for pork belly, short rib–filled lasagna, the "Turducken" Burger, and John's favourite: fresh maple-bacon doughnuts! In the homemade revolution slowly taking hold in Saskatchewan—a place better known for chain restaurants and food that goes from deep freeze to deep fryer—pioneers like chef Mike are leading the masses out of the fast-food desert.

LOCAL GEMS

Outdoor Adult Fitness Circuit

Facing the South Saskatchewan River just beside Victoria Park, Saskatoon's first outdoor adult-fitness circuit is just waiting to be used. Featuring cardio equipment like ellipticals, air walkers, rowing machines, and recumbent bikes, not to mention an agility track, multi-bars, and a variety of press stations, this weatherproof outdoor fitness centre is perfect for anyone who likes to exercise in the great outdoors. Each machine is accompanied by instructions for use. Kiwanis Memorial Park, Spadina Cres. E., Saskatoon, SK, S7K 3G8. www.riverlanding.ca/project_update /phase2/adult-fitness-circuit.

University of Saskatchewan Observatory

Every Saturday night the University of Saskatchewan opens the doors of its observatory to the public for a night of stargazing. On a clear night, and depending on the time of year, expect to see such wonders as star clusters, galaxies, planets, nebulae, and even comets. And even if the weather isn't working in your favour, there's more to explore. You can enjoy educational slideshow presentations of space and beyond as well as tour the museum. 108 Wiggins Rd., Saskatoon, SK, S7N 5E6. www.artsandscience.usask.ca/physics/observatory.

TOFINO, BC

Wildside Grill
Est. 2008
1180 Pacific Rim Highway
Tofino, BC V0R 2Z0
(250) 725-9453
www.wildsidegrill.com

. . . .

The Wildside is a fish lover's dream. Co-owned by fisherman Jeff Mikus and chef Jesse Blake, the Wildside is anything but pretentious. The restaurant boasts only a handful of wooden picnic tables outside, which you're very likely to share with surfers who will regale you with stories of the day's triumphs as you chow down on the Cod Club Sandwich, Oyster Burger, or fish and chips. If you have the hankering, there are even non-fish items, but why break out of the seafood box when it's Wildside fresh?

LOCAL GEM

Tofino Tree Tour

The West Coast is well known for its vast old-growth forests, but did you know that certain trees have names? Tourism Tofino has compiled a list of the top five trees to visit while you're there—some close to 1,500 years old. Located throughout the town and surrounding areas, these trees all have a story to tell. Bust out your GPS and plot a course to check out the must-see trees of Tofino. www.tourismtofino.com/node/150.

WHALE WATCHING   BEAR WATCHING   HOT SPRINGS COVE

Stayin' Alive
How a Guy Who Eats for a Living Stays Above Ground

The first year we shot *You Gotta Eat Here!*, nobody told me I didn't have to eat everything on my plate (Hey, I'm Italian . . . we eat *everything* put in front of us!). So I religiously polished off every plate, bowl, and glass that ventured anywhere near my mouth. Needless to say, the plaid got a bit snug by the end of the season.

I decided things had to change. That's when I elicited the aide of Jim Morrison, my buddy and director on the show. Together, Jim and I decided that as soon as a scene was finished, he would call out, "Put your fork down!" It's a tradition that continues to this day. If I don't obey the order, Jim puffs up his cheeks and arms like a balloon, which usually shames me into stopping.

Jim takes care of me when we're interviewing customers, too. I have a nasty habit of stealing people's fries (because *nothing* tastes as good as a fry from someone else's plate). But every time I do, Jim makes me do squats. Five per fry, to be exact. Thanks, pal. If I end up with an ass like a Norwegian cross-country skier, I'll have you to thank.

The lazy part of me would love squats to be my only exercise, but I've got a wife to look good for, too. So back in 2013 I hired a personal trainer. He put together a few programs for me, which I can do in either the gym or my hotel room. Because even with Jim lording over me, I still manage to stuff an inordinate amount of food into my head every day.

Oh, have I mentioned meals? (Yes, friends, I *do* eat meals—even when we're shooting.) Breakfast is fairly easy, and usually a smoothie in my Bullet blender. I tried to skip lunch for a while but found that my body was still expecting food at that time, plus I would get really hangry (hungry + angry) if I didn't eat. Now I eat salads for lunch, so at least I'm putting something in my gut, though not enough to pop the buttons on my shirts. All bets are off at dinner, especially if we find an Italian restaurant. (What? It's *research*, people.)

As for the leftovers, fear not: We're not throwing anything away. After I'm finished with my part of a dish, the crew steps in. And while they're not like a school of frenzied piranhas, I can certainly see their eyes widen when the fork hits the table. Sometimes—especially if it's a particularly scrumptious dish—the crew will even yell at me to drop my fork.

Hey, maybe *they* should be doing squats, too.

Jim: "Put down the fork, John."
John: "But it's poutine."
Jim: "PUT DOWN THE DAMN FORK, JOHN!"
John: "BUT IT'S POO-TEEN!" Uncomfortable pause. "OK."

The American Cheesesteak Co.
Est. 2011
781 Davie St.
Vancouver, BC V6Z 2S7
(604) 681-0130
www.americancheesesteak.com

Chef Anthony Sedlak was a larger-than-life kind of guy who showed us not only his skill in the kitchen, but a little part of his heart, too. He died suddenly and tragically just a few months after we met him. But his restaurant, owned by friend Andy Eng, continues to serve some of the most authentically delicious cheesesteaks you'll ever eat. Sandwich-loving Vancouverites embrace this American delicacy with a West Coast twist. Try the Classic, the Big Shot, or the New Yorker. Anthony's legend lives on.

Argo Café
Est. 1954
1836 Ontario St.
Vancouver, BC V5T 2W6
(604) 876-3620
www.argocafe.ca

Tiny and eclectic, this neighbourhood institution—run by Denis Larouche and his brother-in-law Kirby Wong—serves gourmet food in a humble setting. Their menu features classic diner food, but the eatery's devotees look first for Denis's daily chalkboard specials, where the magic lies. At the Argo, diner classics and five-star fare coexist peacefully, side by side. It's *the* place in Vancouver for slow food *fast!*

Belgian Fries
Est. 1999
1885 Commercial Dr.
Vancouver, BC V5N 4A6
(604) 253-4220

Historians may fight over whether fries originated in France or Belgium, but Iranian immigrant Ali Faghani is rewriting the history books, mixing the delights of the fried potato with delicious toppings. Try the War Fries, a unique flavour hybrid that hints at the historic Dutch colonization of Indonesia, or take a trip to Northern Africa with Ali's Tunisian Kabob Merguez. There are more poutine options at this globe-trotting foodie destination than you can shake a passport at.

Buckstop
Est. 2013
833 Denman St.
Vancouver, BC V6G 2L7
(604) 428-2528
www.buckstop.ca
· · · · · · · · · · · ·

Craving an over-the-top burger, a Southern barbecue—style brunch, or a special melt topped with tempura bacon?! If you're in Vancouver looking for great barbecue and then some, there's no doubt about it: The Buckstop's here! Once you arrive, follow their motto: Eat meat, repeat. Friday-night regulars know to ask Fiona what the burger will be on Monday

Given the Buckstop's history of mouth-watering burger specials like a brisket-and-hollandaise-stuffed burger topped with fried onions, you'd be excited to get your weekend over with, too!

Calabash Caribbean Bistro
Est. 2010
428 Carrall St.
Vancouver, BC V6B 2J7
(604) 568-5882
www.calabashbistro.com
· · · · · · · · · · · · · · · ·

Chef Cullin David has been cooking Caribbean food since he was five years old. He's putting his experience to good use at Calabash Bistro, making an out-of-this-world jerk sauce and unique specials like the Roti Stack (a pile of delicious Caribbean curry and homemade roti shells). The restaurant is a revolving door for up-and-coming musical acts. Famous hip-hop acts like Wu Tang Clan have been known to stop by for some Calabash jerk chicken! You can, too.

Campagnolo Roma

Est. 2011
2297 Hastings St. E
Vancouver, BC V5L 1V3
(604) 569-0456
www.campagnoloroma.com

You could eat all day at East Van's Campagnolo Roma, which serves up rustic country fare fine enough for a gladiator. This classic peasant food, like their spaghetti al Pomodoro, is made with fresh, quality ingredients by an expert hand.

Chef Joachim Hayward's culinary passion was first ignited in Italy, and the romanticism has stuck with him. Joachim often sings to himself and others as a way of keeping up the good energy when it starts to get hot in the kitchen.

Cannibal Café

Est. 2012
1818 Commercial Dr.
Vancouver, BC V5N 4A5
(604) 558-4199
www.cannibalcafe.ca

Don't let the name fool ya—burgers are the specialty at the Cannibal Café! Celebrate holidays and pop culture with chef Zai Kitagawa's monthly burger specials: Get Stuffed for Thanksgiving with a burgerful of sage stuffing topped with cranberry sauce; Big Popper's patty, filled with jalapeño cream cheese; and A Fish Called Wanda, starring seared albacore tuna. After thirty days it's gone, so eat up! No matter the meat, at Cannibal Café, the burgers have bite.

Cartems Donuterie

Est. 2011
534 West Pender St.
Vancouver, BC V6B 1V3
(778) 708-0996
www.cartems.com

The Cartems Donuterie slogan is "smiles, conversation, and donuts." With flavours like the London Fog, Apple Fritter, and Canadian Whiskey Bacon, Cartems is giving people a lot to smile and talk about. Cartems makes fritters, cakes, and raised yeast doughnuts, and introduces fun new flavour combos all the time. They've been known to use ingredients like local IPAs, Chinese five-spice, and bratwurst. Chef Jordan Cash has an adventurous palate, and he's inviting you to come along with him. Trying new things can be oh-so-sweet!

Chewies Steam & Oyster Bar
Est. 2011
2201 West 1st Ave.
Vancouver, BC V6K 3E6
(604) 558-4448
www.chewies.ca

. . . .

Owned by Richard "Chewie" Chew, Chewies serves up a bevy of bayou classics that even the hardest-core Cajuns adore. Try chef Tyrell Brandvold's Southern Crab Cake Benny, where N'awlins spice meets West Coast groove; the Pulled Short Rib Hash; or one of the equally authentic dinner options. All of them will tickle your taste buds. Whether you choose the Gumbo Yaya or Creole Style Steamers, you'll be taking a trip down South . . . without the humidity.

DD Mau
Est. 2012
1239 Pacific Blvd.
Vancouver, BC V6B 5Z5
(604) 684-4446
www.ddmau.ca

. . . .

Di di mau means "go go quickly!" in Vietnamese, and that's exactly what people are saying about Kim Tran's restaurant—they can't wait to get their hands on her sandwiches! It's in Vancouver's Yaletown area, which is better known for its big box chain restaurants, but Kim decided it was time for something different. DD Mau serves food straight from the heart, and the neighbourhood has responded with open arms. She's making traditional bánh mì sandwiches alongside new twists like crispy roasted pork with crackling and juicy roasted duck. *Di di mau,* indeed!

Deacon's Corner
Est. 2009
3189 West Broadway
Vancouver, BC V6K 2H2
(778) 379-3727
www.deaconscorner.ca

. . . .

Comfort food of the Carolinas meets a retro diner experience on the West Coast. Take a seat in Vancouver's Deacon's Corner for chef

Gabby Hernandez's Southern fried chicken, saucy Carolina pulled pork, or French toast, or have all three in the massive Big Mounties, named to honour the Royal Canadian Mounted Police. Ladies and gentlemen, you have the right to remain stuffed. Some people visit daily just for biscuits. Gabby makes about 700 a month and has the muscles to prove it!

El Camino's
Est. 2010
3250 Main St.
Vancouver, BC V5V 3M5
(604) 875-6246
www.elcaminos.ca

. . . .

Lively, loud, and friendly, El Camino's brings simple yet delicious Latin American street food to Vancouver. But be sure to leave your sombrero at the door, amigo. El Camino's is no stereotype, but a retro-funk joint that combines casual and hip without a sniff of pretense. Head chef Jason Carr

introduces customers to such tongue-tempting delights as arepas, empanadas, and bocadillos. So if you're just going for the food, cancel that ticket to Lima. There's no Machu Picchu in Vancouver, but El Camino's is just as memorable.

La Mezcaleria
Est. 2013
1622 Commercial Dr.
Vancouver, BC V5L 3Y4
(604) 559-8226
www.lamezcaleria.ca

. . . .

It's one big fresh fiesta at La Mezcaleria. They're bringing Mexican food, culture, and theatre straight to the city's East Side. Chef Ignacio Arrieta is originally from Chihuahua, Mexico, and wanted to create a festive environment where people would be comfortable staying long after their meal. The authentic cuisine crafted with traditional techniques makes for a distinctive dining experience you'll never forget. You won't find any nachos grande or chimichangas sullying up this menu, but you might find a mariachi band.

La Taqueria Pinche Taco Shop
Est. 2009
322 West Hastings St.
Vancouver, BC V6B 1K6
(604) 568-4406
www.lataqueria.ca

. . . .

Most people think salsa is the chunky stuff in a jar. Luckily, Marcelo Ramirez Romero's La Taqueria is here to set us straight. It doesn't just taste like the real Mexico; it looks the part, too, with its colourful mural of the Virgin Mary and the Mexican skeleton figurines celebrating Día de los Muertos. So take in the atmosphere and wait for your mouth to be wowed by tacos or quesadillas featuring Marcelo's eleven delicious fillings, which will keep you coming back for a long, long time.

Lucy's Eastside Diner
Est. 2010
2708 Main St.
Vancouver, BC V5T 3E8
(604) 568-1550

· · · · · · · · · · ·

Classic '50s diner, version 2.0. Erv Salvador gives time-honoured diner dishes a totally of-the-moment makeover at Lucy's Eastside Diner in Vancouver. The "kitchen staff get creative" combo dishes jump off the menu at Lucy's. Try the Ian Marshall, an everything-but-the-kitchen-sink hamburger creation named after Erv's best friend's younger brother, or the Mac 'n' Cheese & Meatloaf Hoagie! Open 24/7, this restaurant is a must-visit.

Meet on Main
Est. 2014
4288 Main St.
Vancouver, BC V5V 3P9
(604) 877-1292
www.meetonmain.com

· · · · · · · · · · · · · · · ·

At Meet on Main, chef Linda Antony proves vegan doesn't have to be boring! All your favourite comfort classics are on the menu, like sumptuous smoked burgers, gooey mac 'n' cheese, and nacho fries loaded up with all the fixings. Meet on Main's not just for vegetarians—this business is buzzing every day of the week with meat lovers and veg-heads alike! With so many inventive dishes on the menu, we promise you won't miss the meat at Meet on Main.

Neighbour's Restaurant
Est. 1982
6493 Victoria Dr.
Vancouver, BC V5P 3X5
(604) 327-1456
www.neighboursrestaurant.ca

· · · · · · · · · · · · · · · · · · ·

Owned by the Tsoukas family, this is one of the most welcoming restaurants you'll ever set foot in, thanks partly to Papa George, the lovable patriarch who feels like everyone's dad. George instantly connects with people, whether it's by rubbing their shoulders after a long workday or by warming their bellies with his signature Greek and Italian recipes, including thirty-five varieties of pizza. Want a one-way ride to the Acropolis? Try George's roast lamb, a fall-off-the-bone dish that Aristotle himself would love!

Nuba
Est. 2003
146 East 3rd Ave.
Vancouver, BC V5T 1C8
(604) 568-6727
www.nuba.ca

· · · · · · · · · ·

At Nuba, the bright and flavourful Lebanese recipes have been passed down through generations of Bouzide family members and right onto your plate. Who knew falafel could taste this good—or historic? Victor Bouzide's great-grandmother served the same recipe at the 1893 World's Fair in Chicago. Chef Ernesto Gomez knows that simple is best. He worked at Paris's Ritz Hotel and a Michelin three-star restaurant in Spain, but now he's traded in all the fuss for straightforward Lebanese cooking with soul! Vancouverites love him for it.

Panaderia Latina Bakery
Est. 2004
4906 Joyce St.
Vancouver, BC V5R 4G6
(604) 439-1414

· · · · · · · · · ·

A visit to Panaderia Latina Bakery takes you to Chile for lunch without ever leaving East Van. Fill up on a big, meaty Chilean sandwich called a chacarero, dig into a freshly baked empanada, or go straight to dessert with a sweet slice of milhoja, a puff pastry delight. And when your clumsy English tongue tries to order just about anything in the bakery, chef Leslie Riquelme is as patient and sweet as the goods she bakes.

Rangoli

Est. 2004
1480 West 11th Ave.
Vancouver, BC V6H 3H8
(604) 736-5711
www.vijsrangoli.ca

. . . .

Rangoli is Vikram Vij's vision of a bustling Bombay restaurant in the middle of Vancouver. Although Vikram is known for pushing boundaries with Indian-style pulled pork, he also does the classics just right! In this friendly and casual spot, Vikram uses traditional Indian spices and recipes but adds local twists like dousing portobello mushrooms in creamy curry sauce or piling spicy pulled pork on sautéed greens. Rangoli regulars can't eat curry anywhere else now.

The Reef Restaurant

Est. 1999
4172 Main St.
Vancouver, BC V5V 3P7
(604) 874-5375
www.thereefrestaurant.com

. . . .

At the Reef, the Caribbean way of life (and dining) is alive and well, even when the thermometer dips below zero outside. Every menu item is a tribute to Liz de Mata and Simon Cotton's vision, as owners, and chef Paulette's skill. Enjoy the West Indian roti, jerk chicken

poutine, or ackee and saltfish, the national dish of Jamaica. If you're surprised by the relaxed groove slowly washing over you, settle in . . . you'll get used to it.

Romer's Burger Bar

Est. 2010
1873 West 4th Ave.
Vancouver, BC V6J 1M4
(604) 732-9545
www.romersburgerbar.com

. . . .

Jim Romer of Romer's Bar is elevating burgers to new heights with delicious innovations like lettuce-wrapped chorizo burgers, crispy onions piled sky-high, and beef burgers topped with heaps of succulent braised short ribs. (That's right, it's meat on top of more meat!) All of Romer's burgers are served with a side of Jim's grandma's famous garlic olives. People can't get enough! Jim had to start offering this signature snack by the jar for people to take home.

Scandilicious

Deacon's Corner

La Mezcaleria

Albacore Tuna Ceviche (La Mezcaleria)

Romer's Burger Bar

Pulled Pork (Rangoli)

Noodle-y Thai (Meet on Main)

El Camino's

Lucy's Eastside Diner

The Reef Restaurant

Man's Man Burger (Romer's Burger Bar)

Scandilicious
Est. 2012
25 Victoria Dr.
Vancouver, BC V5L 2T6
(604) 877-2277
www.scandilicious.com

Break out the Viking horns because Scandilicious is serving delicious Scandinavian specialities like kumle potato dumplings, Norwegian meatballs, and smørrebrød waffle sandwiches. Mother-daughter team Anita and Kristina Cotton wanted their restaurant to have a family feel and are proud to know their customer's names and orders by heart! They've hung up a great big "*Velkommen*" sign, and Anita even built all the furniture herself in their Viking-themed dining room. Come on in!

Slickity Jim's Chat & Chew
Est. 1997
3475 Main St.
Vancouver, BC V5V 3M9
(604) 873-6760
www.slickityjims.com

Slickity Jim's is the granddaddy of joints that warm your heart. It's so well loved that when the building burnt down in 2010, locals threw a benefit concert to kick-start its renaissance. Firmly ensconced in the big city, Slickity Jim's pays homage to chef Mike Zalman's love of small-town diners. Can't decide where to start? Order the Abstract Notion, a dish that changes according to Mike's gourmet-inspired whims. It's different and delicious every time. At this *You Gotta Eat Here!* Fan Favourite, fun is always on the menu.

The Tomahawk
Est. 1926
1550 Philip Ave.
North Vancouver, BC V7P 2V8
(604) 988-2612
www.tomahawkrestaurant.com

Since becoming Vancouver's first drive-in restaurant in 1926, the Tomahawk has built a reputation for belly-warming food, mountainous portions, and an interior design that straddles the fine line between museum and urban kitsch. The decor is testimony to the Chamberlain family's fascination with the culture of First Nations people of the West Coast, with whom founder Chick traded food for objects during the Depression. Now Chick's son Chuck offers burgers named after chiefs and other delicious dishes. Visit this must-see restaurant for a taste of a living legend.

Topanga Café
Est. 1978
2904 West 4th Ave.
Vancouver, BC V6K 4A9
(604) 733-3713
www.topangacafe.ca

. . . .

The Topanga combines a funky atmosphere with creative cooking to give Vancouverites an authentic south-of-the-border experience. It's boisterous and busy, thanks to dedicated locals who know you're guaranteed a superb meal every visit. And if that meal includes the Wet Prawn Burrito, all the better! Another favourite Topanga specialty is the Carne Norteña (Meat of the North). Need a little sugar? Try the Homemade Chocolate Cake. Okay, it's not covered in avocado sauce, but we'll let them slide on this one.

Via Tevere Pizzeria
Est. 2012
1190 Victoria Dr.
Vancouver, BC V5L 4G5
(604) 336-1803
www.viateverepizzeria.com

. . . .

Eating here is like a trip to the old country. Want proof? Frank and Dominic Morra's Via Tevere was one of *the first* restaurants in Canada to be certified by the Associazione Vera Pizza Napoletana, which safeguards the cultural heritage of Italy's most famous export. Want more? The place is named after the Naples street where Frank and Dom's dad grew up. Still skeptical? Via Tevere's wood-burning oven is imported directly from Naples! Sold! Try the Margherita, the Filetto, or the Capricciosa pizza.

The Wallflower Modern Diner
Est. 2009
2420 Main St.
Vancouver, BC V5T 3E2
(604) 568-7554
www.thewallflowermoderndiner.com

. . . .

Owner and chef Lisa Skelton definitely didn't name the Wallflower after herself. She's the one in the Hello Kitty short shorts and go-go boots, cooking up eats sure to please all your peeps. No wonder this "place where cool kids take their parents" is a *You Gotta Eat Here!* Fan Favourite. Its old-school comfort classics with modern twists include lots of vegetarian, vegan, and gluten-free options. Try the Meatloaf Wellington or the Tofu Rancheros. Here, everyone's a member of one big, quirky, and totally awesome family.

Yolk's

Est. 2013
1298 East Hastings St.
Vancouver, BC V6A 1S6
(604) 428-9655
www.yolks.ca

· · · · · · · · · · ·

Yolk's cracks a thousand eggs every Sunday so you don't have to crack yours! Using culinary techniques like braising, smoking, and confit, chef Steve Ewing pairs breakfast staples like Benedicts with double-smoked bacon or BC smoked sockeye salmon for an all-day breakfast adventure. From the French toast to chicken and waffles, their rotating specials make Yolk's a breakfast destination for their regulars. Steve spends hours making your breakfast, but don't worry—he understands if you eat it in seconds.

Campagnolo Roma

DD Mau

Pancakes (Yolk's)

Cannibal Café

Buckstop

Nuba

Cartems Donuterie

Eggs Benedict (Yolk's)

LOCAL GEMS

Lynn Canyon Suspension Bridge

Not quite as big as Vancouver's most famous suspension bridge (which crosses the Capilano River), the 50-metre-high Lynn Canyon Suspension Bridge offers a fun and exhilarating but less crowded experience. Located in Lynn Valley, the bridge sways and bounces while you walk across. If your nerves don't get to you, be sure to stop in the middle to take in the breathtaking view of the canyon and surrounding forest. www.lynncanyon.ca/tour/suspension-bridge.

Prohibition City Walking Tours

In 1917, Prohibition was introduced to Vancouver, initiating an illicit world of bootlegged booze and rum-running. The Prohibition City walking tour will take you on a historical journey through the streets of Vancouver, highlighting the most illustrious locations from the city's storied past. This 1-hour-and-45-minute tour features stories you'll be hard-pressed to find anywhere else. Tickets are $25 for adults and $22 for students and seniors, and tours run throughout the year. Meeting point: Cathedral Square, 566 Richards St., Vancouver, BC, V6B 1X4. www.forbiddenvancouver.ca/prohibition-city-walking-tour.

The Sam Kee Building

Listed by the *Guinness Book of World Records* as the world's narrowest freestanding office building, the Sam Kee Building on Pender St. is only 6 feet 2 inches deep. In 1912, the City of Vancouver widened Pender St., which reclaimed 24 feet of the above-ground property. Chang Toy, owner of the Sam Kee Company, refused to let this faze him and hired architects Kennerly Bryan and William C.F. Gillam to design the steel-frame building. Today it operates as an insurance office. 8 West Pender St., Vancouver, BC, V6B 1R3.

VanDusen Garden's Elizabethan Hedge Maze

Get your compass out and try not to get lost in VanDusen Garden's Elizabethan Hedge Maze. One of only six in North America, the maze was planted in 1981 and has been groomed over the years into a work of art. It uses 3000 pyramidal cedars to create the maze walls and is one of the focal points of the 55-acre garden it inhabits. 5251 Oak St., Vancouver, BC, V6M 4H1. www.vandusengarden.org/explore/vandusen-botanical-garden.

The Marine Building

Built between 1929 and 1930, the Marine Building's stunning art deco architecture makes it one of the most beautiful and decadent buildings in the city. It has served as a filming location for multiple projects including *Smallville*, *Blade: Trinity*, *Time Cop*, *Fantastic Four*, and *Fantastic Four: Rise of the Silver Surfer*. Breathtaking both inside and out, this building is a photo op waiting to happen. Be sure to check out the intricate terra cotta cameos depicting the discovery of the Pacific Coast. 355 Burrard St., Vancouver, BC, V6C 0B2. www.vancouverarchitecture.mikepriebe .ca/marine-building.

VICTORIA, BC

Bin 4 Burger Lounge
Est. 2011
716 Goldstream Ave., #102
Langford, BC V98 2X3
(778) 265-5464
www.bin4burgerlounge.com

. . . .

Bin 4 is the place in Victoria to get over-the-top burger creations. Bin 4 Burger Lounge's cool and laid-back atmosphere makes it the perfect place to meet up with friends and grab an after-work burger. Walking, talking burger manual Mike Ringland makes sensationally delicious burgers using simply seasoned patties and a whack of creative, homemade condiments to add bold personality. With seven different aiolis, homemade relishes, mustards, ketchups, and a signature bourbon barbecue sauce, Bin 4 is sure to impress!

Ferris' Oyster Bar
Est. 1991
536 Yates St.
Victoria, BC V8W 1K8
(250) 360-1824
www.ferrisoysterbar.com

. . . .

Land lubbin' is highly overrated—at least that's what folks at Ferris' will tell you. Want a salmon burger so fresh you can almost taste the ocean? Any seafarer would be happy with chef Merlin Hind's pick of oysters—raw, steamed, or smoked. You'll slurp those suckers down. Located in one of Victoria's oldest buildings from the 1850s, Ferris' serves the best of the sea's bounty on ship or shore with every manner of sea creature on the menu!

Floyd's Diner
Est. 2006
866 Yates St.
Victoria, BC V8W 1L8
(250) 381-5114
www.floydsdiner.ca

. . . .

At Floyd's, the all-day breakfasts and lunches are as heavy on humour as they are on calories, and it's all thanks to owner Petr Prusa. Try the Berlin Wall Omelette ("When you knock this down, you'll feel liberated") or the First Kiss Burger ("sorta wet, sloppy, and awkward at first, but ultimately something you'll remember forever"). Feel daring? Gamble on the Mahoney, which is whatever the chef dreams up at that particular moment. If you're not happy, you can always flip for it . . . double or nothin'!

FOO Asian Street Food
Est. 2009
769 Yates St.
Victoria, BC V8W 1L6
(250) 383-3111
www.foofood.ca
. . . .

Chef Patrick Lynch takes Asian street food flavours indoors at FOO. He brings his inventive flair to familiar takeout staples, using braised short ribs in his beef and broccoli chow mein, and adding succulent deep-fried pork belly to his sweet and sour pork. Chef Patrick's dream was to become a rock star, but his parents told him to have a back-up plan. Luckily for Victoria food fans, his other dream was to perform as a cook! You'd be a FOO not to eat here!

Jam Café
Est. 2012
542 Herald St.
Victoria, BC V8W 1S5
(778) 440-4489
www.jamcafes.com/victoria
. . . .

Jam's whimsical menu will bring out your playful side! At this inviting home away from home, they whip up wondrous dishes like teetering triple-layered huevos rancheros and spicy pulled pork pancakes crowned with pickled red cabbage. The playful brunch menu is dear to owners Jim and Candy Walmsley's hearts. Dishes like Green Eggs and Ham and the Three Pigs are inspired by their kids, after whom the Charlie Bowl, the Harrison, and the Cracker Jack are named.

John's Place Restaurant
Est. 1984
723 Pandora Ave.
Victoria, BC V8W 1N9
(250) 389-0711
www.johnsplace.ca
. . . .

Owner and master chef John Cantin (who represented Canada at the 1976 World Culinary Olympics) wows loyal customers with ten varieties of eggs Benny and other delicious specialties. John's feel-good energy is everywhere, from the menu to the interior design, and nothing makes him happier

than seeing you enjoy his food.
A major fave is the Cloudy with a
Chance of Meatloaf.

Pagliacci's
Est. 1979
1011 Broad St.
Victoria, BC V8W 2A1
(250) 386-1662
www.pagliaccis.ca

. . . .

At Pagliacci's, the only things larger
than the portions are the characters
who run the joint, Brooklyn natives
David and Howie Siegel. Howie says
he is the face of Pagliacci's, while
his brother is the backside—in a
voice that rings loudly throughout
this jam-packed piece of pasta
heaven, one of the best Italian
joints we've encountered. Try the
delicious Big Easy and the Heming-
way Short Story. For dessert, there's
New York cheesecake ("the dish
that made us . . . and Manhattan").

Pig BBQ Joint
Est. 2007
1325 Blanshard St.
Victoria, BC V8W 3S2
(250) 590-5193
www.pigbbqjoint.com

. . . .

Pig BBQ Joint started as a small
sandwich counter with an offsite
smoker, but it's now a full-fledged
restaurant superstar thanks to
its daily specials, like the Bacon
Explosion Sandwich—Pig BBQ's
legendary over-the-top bacon roll.
Chef and owner Jeff Hetherington
encourages his staff to create the
out-of-this-world specials that
make Pig BBQ Joint famous. Jeff
also indulges the inner child with
a side dish of fried mac 'n' cheese
and the option of an ice-cream
float as part of a meal deal!

The Pink Bicycle
Est. 2007
1008 Blanshard St.
Victoria, BC V8W 2H5
(250) 384-1008
www.pinkbicycleburger.com

. . . .

The Pink Bicycle has some of
Victoria's best burgers. Along
with being a relatable symbol for
Victoria's hippy crowd, the bright
pink bike in the window is the
very same bike that owner Morgan
Hradecky rode through the desert
during a Burning Man festival.
Luckily you won't need to head out

Pig BBQ Joint

FOO Asian Street Food

Swiss Mushroom Almond Burger
(ReBar Modern Food)

Chef Megan Turner (ReBar Modern Food)

Jam Café

to the desert to trip out. Your mind will be blown by their whacked-out burgers and sides.

ReBar Modern Food
Est. 1988
50 Bastion Sq.
Victoria, BC V8W 1J2
(250) 361-9223
. . . .

ReBar is named after the reinforcing steel that makes a building strong, and their food will do the same for your body, from the inside out. Chef Megan Turner dishes up decadent vegetarian comfort food with layers of unexpected flavour. She doesn't replicate meat dishes in vegetarian form. Highlighting beauty without the beef, she draws inspiration from cultural cuisine around the world to create food that stands on its own without needing modified veggie proteins to trick your tongue. Megan is a true master of meatlessness.

Shine Café
Est. 2004
1548 Fort St.
Victoria, BC V8S 5J2
(250) 595-2133
www.shinecafe.ca
. . . .

Barry Thomson is one of John's favourite chefs, restaurant owners, and people. Yeah, he whips up adventurous brunch dishes that people line up for. But what makes Barry truly extraordinary is the love he puts into his food, his life, and Shine Café. This place is a Benny lover's dream, in large part due to Barry's seven kinds of hollandaise sauce. Crave sweets? Try the Eiffel Tower of French toast. Inventiveness is always on the menu at Shine.

Tibetan Kitchen Café

Est. 2008
680 Broughton St.
Victoria, BC V8W 2C9
(250) 383-5664
www.tibetankitchen.com

. . . .

The world is a much smaller place than it used to be. How else can you explain a restaurant owned by a woman born in India to Tibetan parents, who met her Canadian husband on a cruise ship in international waters and settled in Victoria? Now those are the ingredients for one spicy curry! Pemba Bhatia expertly blends culinary influences. Her shepta (a Tibetan-style stir-fry) is a prime example. So too are her samosas, served with curried onion rings. The world may be small, but these flavours are big!

The Village Restaurant

Est. 2007
2518 Estevan Ave.
Victoria, BC V8R 2S7
(250) 592-8311
www.thevillagerestaurant.ca

. . . .

The Village is a Victoria institution, serving up Jewish-inspired brunches with latkes and smoked salmon. When Jason and Barry Chan bought the place, they painted a giant orange map of the neighbourhood on the ceiling as a tribute. Several menu items are named after prominent Victoria landmarks, like the Blue Bridge and the Mount Douglas omelettes. They also follow the sellers' one piece of advice: serve bacon!

LOCAL GEMS

Abkhazi Garden

When the Georgian Prince and Princess Abkhazi settled down in Victoria, BC, in 1946, they began building a garden that would truly represent the spirit of the city. Though you can't ascertain its beauty from the street, when you enter the one-acre property you will be greeted by a sight that uses Victoria's natural rocky landscape as the canvas for a stunning garden display. Considered by the Abkhazis to be their child, the garden has been more than fifty years in the making. 1964 Fairfield Rd., Victoria, BC, V8S 1H2. blog.conservancy.bc.ca/properties /vancouver-island-region/abkhazi-garden.

Craigdarroch Castle

Designed with the intention of using the grandiose castle to flaunt family wealth and launch the unmarried Dunsmuir daughters into society, patriarch Robert Dunsmuir ordered the construction of the castle in 1887. Sadly, he died in 1889, one year before it was completed. The castle still stands as a testament to the privileged lifestyle of the Scottish immigrant family, which can be seen throughout the impressive building in its stunning stained-glass windows, detailed woodwork, and classy Victorian-era furnishings. 1050 Joan Cres., Victoria, BC, V8S 3L5. www.thecastle.ca.

Victoria Butterfly Gardens

The Victoria Butterfly Gardens offer a tropical paradise with up to seventy different species of butterflies, but that's not all you'll find when wandering through the jungle paths. Iguanas, tortoises, flamingos, tropical ducks, macaws, koi fish, poison dart frogs, and more await your discovery. The gardens also feature a large variety of tropical flowers, fruits from around the world, and carnivorous plants. Bonus: See if you can spot the chameleons hiding among the trees! 1461 Benvenuto Ave., Brentwood Bay, BC, V8M 1R3. www.butterflygardens.com.

Fan Tan Alley

Though the Fan Tan Alley you'll see today is home to boutique shops selling their wares, it possesses quite the sordid history. Named after a popular gambling game played there during the early 1940s, *fan* meaning "turn over" and *tan* meaning "spread out," the narrow alleyway was home to all sorts of debauchery in its heyday, including opium dens and gambling rings. It also holds the record for the narrowest street in Canada (between 3 and 6 feet wide), which makes it one of Victoria's most interesting local gems. Connects Fisgard St. and Pandora Ave. between Government St. and Store St. www.chinatown.library.uvic.ca/fan_tan_alley.

Victoria's Crowning Glory
My Most Memorable Place to Visit

I have a confession: When it came to deciding the most memorable place I've visited, I struggled a bit . . . but probably not for the reasons you think. You see, the problem here is that I've visited *so many* amazing places that narrowing it down to just one was almost impossible. Would it be Florence or Vancouver? Toronto or Dublin? And no offense to you Londonites, but as much as I loved warming my cockles in your great city, the more I thought about it, the more I realized that Victoria tops my list.

Why?

First of all, Victoria is stunningly beautiful. The city sits right on the water (that's the Strait of Georgia, for you geographic types), and its Inner Harbour is one of the most pleasant places I've ever been, especially in the summer when it's the focus of festivals, shows, and music. You can buy handmade art, turn around and watch a busker perform, then go grab a gelato while you watch the float planes come and go across the water. And, hey, if walking's not your thing, they even have little tugboat-style water-taxis that will take you to lots of cool places around the harbour.

As a guy who spends long hours shooting inside, I'm a big fan of walkable cities, and Victoria is as pedestrian-friendly as it gets. It helps that the place is one of the warmest spots in Canada, right? I mean, even when it's cold, it's not cold in Victoria (sorry, Whitehorse).

And have I mentioned the food? Well, please allow me to, because this is where Victoria shines. Call me a creature of habit, but there are restaurants I visit every time we're in Victoria. Whether it's Pagliacci's (So it's an Italian place? So what? Stop!), Shine Café, or John's Place, we are never short on culinary destinations here. (*Psst* . . . don't tell anyone I said this, but there's a pizza joint in Victoria—Pizzeria Prima Strada—that's never been on *You Gotta Eat Here!* but *still* has some of the best pizza in the country.)

The people? They're lovely, too. And really, how can they not be? With everything this little city has going for it, it's hard not to walk around with a big pizza-eatin' grin on your face.

Victoria's cool vibe doesn't just live in its harbour. The downtown core is peppered with amazing shops; you can spend days wandering around and never get bored.

Bistro Dansk Restaurant
Est. 1977
63 Sherbrook St.
Winnipeg, MB R3C 2B2
(204) 775-5662
www.bistrodansk.com

. . . .

Czech owner and chef Paul Vocadlo has been cooking Danish dishes like schnitzel, kylling, and frikadeller (hey, can we actually say that in print?) for more than twenty years, and he's damn good at it! While you're sure to get a taste of Europe at Bistro Dansk, not everything is Danish. Paul's palachinkas and a few other specialties are a tribute to his Czech heritage. Add it all together and you've got an international range of reasons to stop by the family-run Bistro Dansk.

Boon Burger Café
Est. 2010
79 Sherbrook St.
Winnipeg, MB R3C 2B2
(204) 415-1391
www.boonburger.ca

. . . .

When you whip up tasty, crispy, and exotic blends like the vegan Boon Burger Café does, it doesn't matter if you're an herbivore, an omnivore, or a carnivore. Nobody ever leaves dissatisfied . . . or hungry! Voted Winnipeg's best burger in 2010, Anneen duPlessis and Tomas Sohlberg's little eatery welcomes everyone with a taste for the extraordinary. Enjoy the Thanksgiving Burger, gluten-free Bombay Heat Burger, or Not the Same Ol' Poutine. At the Boon Burger, the unexpected is expected.

Kawaii Crepe

Est. 2009
99 Osborne St., #201
Winnipeg, MB R3L 2R4
(204) 415-2833
www.kawaiicrepe.ca

. . . .

The versatile crêpe is always full of surprises. Here's one: they're not just from France! Candy Lam and Phil Salazar's Kawaii Crepe specializes in *kurépu*, a Japanese take on a classic European dish. The place is funky and fun, and more reminiscent of Japanese anime than a traditional Canadian café. Kawaii makes enough fillings to satisfy every taste from Tokyo to, well, Winnipeg. Try the Pump Up the Yam, the Big Feast, the Ninja Crêpe, or It's-a-Smore.

Marion Street Eatery

Est. 2014
393 Marion St.
Winnipeg, MB R2H 0V4
(204) 233-2843
www.marionstreeteatery.com

. . . .

At Winnipeg's Marion Street Eatery, co-owners Laneil Smith and Melissa Hryb make sure everybody leaves happy and full, with their chummy, neighbourly service and deliciously elevated comfort classics. Tired of cooking at places where her family couldn't afford to eat, Melissa brought her upscale culinary chops to create a soulful menu of down-home dishes like chili with crispy local onions, and house-baked bannock and meatloaf stuffed with cheese and spinach. And yes, they're as tasty as they sound.

NuBurger

Est. 2012
472 Stradbrook Ave.
Winnipeg, MB R3L 0J9
(204) 888-1001
www.ilovenuburger.com

. . . .

Fresh, fun, gourmet, and oh so *goooooood*, NuBurger's got it all. Taking the classic burger and throwing international toppings on it, this place is keeping Winnipeg fed with inventive ways to make the good old burger Nu again. Chef Ivan Valencia crafts an eating experience that satisfies both tongue and tummy. NuBurger's burgers are made so the average Joe can wrap his mitts around them and sing their praises. Try the Blueberry Yum Yum or the Shangh Awesome.

Red Top Drive-Inn Restaurant

Est. 1960
219 St. Mary's Rd.
Winnipeg, MB R2H 1J2
(204) 233-7943
www.redtopdriveinn.com

. . . .

There may not be waitresses in roller skates delivering your food to your car anymore, but traditions are alive and well at the family-run Red Top Drive-Inn. From the red vinyl booths to the fried chicken and burgers, the Red Top is a delicious and comforting trip back in time. Owner Pete Scouras works hard to meet the made-from-scratch standard that his ancestors built, serving up Greek dishes from his heritage as well as classic diner fare. Come to the Red Top and start your own family tradition.

Summit Café

Est. 2013
23 Main St.
Stony Mountain, MB R0C 3A0
(204) 344-0205
www.summitcafe.ca

. . . .

Nadine Dannenberg's Summit Café is a family-run eclectic eatery that's like nothing the locals have ever seen. Everyone's swooning over the inventive twists on classic diner comfort food coming out of the kitchen, like the BLT with Bacon Marmalade. These dishes could easily find a home on any metropolitan menu, but are an unexpected thrill in Stony Mountain. Climb that hill and get your fill!

The Tallest Poppy

Est. 2007
103 Sherbrook St.
Winnipeg, MB R3B 1E1
(204) 219-8777
www.thetallestpoppy.com

. . . .

Talia Syrie's retro-chic café, where classic Jewish cooking gets new life, has many customers making the pilgrimage for a bowl of chicken matzo ball soup and some blintzes. Try Talia's Chicken Fried Steak and Eggs, which features her mother's brisket recipe, or the bison meatloaf, proof that Talia isn't afraid to tinker with tradition. A popular combination of old and new, it's like Saturday afternoon at your bubbe's house.

LOCAL GEMS

Cement Cemetery

The purpose and origins of one of Winnipeg's strangest landmarks are heavily debated by locals. The collection of concrete spires colloquially known as the "Cement Cemetery," likely the remnants of concrete testing, features numbers etched into the pillars. Believed to have been constructed in the 1950s or '60s, the abstract monument is a mysterious sight to behold and not to be missed if you're drawn to the weird and unexplainable. Sturgeon Rd., north of Inkster Blvd.

Longitudinal Centre of Canada

Some people will argue that the longitudinal centre of Canada is still up for debate, but the point established by the country is about a half-hour drive southeast of Winnipeg. Signs sit on both sides of the Trans-Canada Highway marking the halfway point measured from the farthest outlying islands on either coast. Mark Canada's halfway point with a celebratory photo op and decide which half of Canada to travel to next. GPS coordinates: 96°38'45"W (49.76773 -96.8097).

Manitoba's Iceland

If you've ever wanted to travel to Iceland but don't want to spend hours on a plane to get there, you can find a little piece of it closer to home. The Manitoba community of Gimli, located just off the wet shore of Lake Winnipeg, was settled by Icelanders in 1875 and has preserved Iceland's culture and language ever since. It is also home to the Icelandic Festival of Manitoba, or "Islendingadagurinn," believed to be the second-oldest continuous cultural festival in Canada. www.gimli.ca.

@#$%&! Potty Mouth
And Other Bloopers That Occasionally Get in the Way of an Otherwise Civilized TV Program

I never swear.

Scratch that.

I never swear on TV.

Closer.

I often swear. It just never makes it past the editors.

Nailed it.

I know, I know . . . it's a family show. But when you're an Italian guy outta Toronto, swearing is almost a way of life (sorry, Ma). Couple that with eating amazing food day in and day out, and you have a recipe for the occasional slip of the tongue.

Can you blame me? You know what it's like when you take a bite of something absolutely delicious. You cradle that burger or sandwich in your hands, a glazed look washes over your face, and all you want to say is "Wow. That's just f**king delicious." Well . . . I do that. Sometimes.

By now, the crew is used to my occasionally R-rated language. They just shrug and keep the cameras rolling because they know I just *have to* get it out. But once I'm done, I realize the error of my ways and jump into the family-friendly retake. Things get a little stickier when I'm working with a fellow Italian who appreciates a good cuss as much as I do. That's when the crew sits down and gets comfortable—they know it's going to be a while.

Occasionally, I get thrown a massive curveball that demands all my self-control. The biggest challenge came in Season 5, when we shot episodes with kids. Forget about the occasional slip-up—I had to stay clean *all day*! Okay, so maybe I couldn't help myself. But I just told the kids the same thing I tell my own daughters: I'm an adult and I can use these words, just like you'll be able to when you're adults.

But for all the stigma that surrounds swearing on TV, I find that it occasionally comes in handy, especially when I'm working with a nervous chef or owner who's never appeared on camera before. That's when I take them aside, look at them gravely, and say, "Now whatever you do, don't f**k up."

No, it never makes it to air. But it sure helps break the ice.

WTF? Oh yeah, a string of swear words accompanied this little modelling session. Luckily, there were no kids in the room. What else is a guy in a frilly apron supposed to do?

CENTRAL
CANADA

COLLINGWOOD, ON

The Iron Skillet
Est. 1989
20 Balsam St., #2
Collingwood, ON L9Y 4H7
(705) 444-5804
www.theironskillet.ca

See what's cookin' at the Iron Skillet, a twenty-five-year-old Collingwood institution run by the zany Tony Sensenberger. At the very least, you're in for a hearty home-cooked meal, but real die-hard Skilleters look to the daily feature menu for adventurous international dishes like spicy chicken enchiladas, jambalaya, and traditional paella. Even though Tony works in the back kitchen, regulars here know him personally. You'll come back for the food, and you'll linger a little longer for the company!

The Smoke
Est. 2012
498 First St.
Collingwood, ON L9Y 3J2
(705) 293-5522
www.thesmoke.ca

Owner Cam Dyment received a smoker from his father-in-law for his birthday and it changed his life. Now Collingwood locals and vacationers rave about Cam's smoked burgers, ribs, and pulled pork. It takes two hours to get those burgers perfectly tender and smoky, and Cam finishes them up sous vide to lock in all that moisture. It may be untraditional, but folks say Cam's burgers are some of the juiciest you'll ever try! Make sure to save room for his smoked desserts, like his apple crisp and smoked banana ice cream.

Paella (The Iron Skillet)

Ribs (The Smoke)

Chef Cam Dyment
(The Smoke)

LOCAL GEMS

Explore a Cave

Scenic Caves Nature Adventures offers a wide variety of outdoor activities, from a 420-foot-long suspension bridge to guided nighttime snowshoeing, treetop walks, zip-lining, and, of course, cave exploration. These caves were carved out of the earth by glacial ice millions of years ago. The scenic caves will take you to the highest point of the Niagara Escarpment, one of Canada's sixteen UNESCO world biosphere reserves. 260/280 Scenic Caves Rd., The Blue Mountains, ON, L9Y 0P2. www.sceniccaves.com.

Ridge Runner Mountain Coaster

It's a known fact that Collingwood is famous for its skiing options, but what you might not know is that you can hit the slopes in a different way during the spring and summer months. The Ridge Runner Mountain Coaster allows you to explore 1 kilometre of Blue Mountain terrain in a roller-coaster-like cart that glides securely along a metal track. Glide at your own pace or go up to 42 kilometres per hour if you're more daring. Just be sure to take in all the greenery before it's covered up with snow. Blue Mountain Resort, 108 Jozo Weider Blvd., The Blue Mountains, ON, L9Y 3Z2. www.bluemountain.ca/things-to-do/activities/ridge-runner-coaster.

GATINEAU, QC

Edgar
Est. 2010
60 rue Bégin
Gatineau, QC J9A 1C8
(819) 205-1110
www.chezedgar.ca

. . . .

Chef Marysol Foucault is one of those rare personalities who lives for what she does. At Edgar, the tiny and intimate restaurant that bears her father's name, people feel like they are part of a kinder, simpler time. Though the place is a throwback to the '50s and '60s, the recipes are 100% cutting-edge, spinning old favourites into modern-day works of art. Enjoy La Bûcheronne ("Lady Lumberjack"), the Fig Sandwich, and the famous Lemon Beignets. You won't want to leave a restaurant as lovely as this.

LOCAL GEM

Catch a Show at Cabaret a Basoche

This 120-seat theatre offers a wonderful variety of plays, concerts, and more for the visitors and residents of Gatineau. Located in a beautiful heritage building, the auditorium provides entertainment for all ages. With over eighty shows passing through the theatre each year, you're sure to find something exciting onstage when you visit. The theatre also features a gallery, Espace Pierre-Debain, which often showcases visual arts exhibitions and unique arts and crafts projects. 120 rue Principale, Gatineau, QC, J9H 3M3. www.gatineau.ca/portail/default.aspx?p=quoi_faire/spectacles_theatre.

GUELPH, ON

Baker Street Station
Est. 2011
76 Baker St.
Guelph, ON N1H 4G1
(519) 265-7960
www.bakerstreetstation.ca

Chef Brett MacDonald is all about
fun and adventurous eating at
Guelph's Baker Street Station. The
restaurant's name is a nod to the
London Underground, and the
menu is true to its working-class
roots. Brett keeps his curious
customers coming back for his
surprisingly delicious twists on
everyday dishes—think Pad Thai
Fries, or Braised Octopus and
Nduja Tacos! The Baker Street
Station puts a fresh spin on the
traditional English pub experience.
Relax and dig in!

Black Forest Inn
Est. 1967
255 King St. E
Hamilton, ON L8N 1B9
(905) 528-3538
www.blackforestinn.ca

. . . .

Nothing warms you up on a winter day like schnitzel. The success of Hamilton's Black Forest Inn says that many other people feel the same. This family-run Canadian legend has been comforting customers with old-world, stick-to-your-ribs classics since Fred and Rosa Oberreiter founded it decades ago. Son Wolfgang Schoen and his wife, Gabi, run it now, offering thirteen types of schnitzel.

Burger Barn
Est. 2011
3000 Fourth Line
Ohsweken, Six Nations of the Grand River Reserve, ON N0A 1M0
(519) 445-0088
www.burgerbarn.ca

. . . .

The Burger Barn is a joint whose energy and vitality have built a reputation far beyond its borders. The Barn is the brainchild of the Hill family, who lamented the few dining options on Canada's largest reserve. With Burger Barn, they brought the best of old-school diner food home. Big appetites go for the Barnyard burger, which walks the fine line between girth and flavour, or the well-loved Indian Taco, made with frybread. If you're looking for hand-held heaven, the Barn is a must-visit.

The Burnt Tongue
Est. 2013
10 Cannon St. E
Hamilton, ON L8L 1Z5
(905) 536-1146
www.theburnttongue.com

. . . .

For comfort in every spoonful, head to the Burnt Tongue, where chef Dan Robinson offers up three wildly inventive soups on his daily menu, serving over 250 litres every day! With soup as Dan's medium for exploring every food trend and cuisine on the map, his ever-changing menu is driven by local ingredients. Try Spiced Coconut and Parsnip Soup with Walnuts or his Moqueca South American Fish Soup. Whichever you choose, it's guaranteed to be *souper* delicious!

Chicago Style Pizza Shack
Est. 1975
534 Upper Sherman Ave.
Hamilton, ON L8V 3M1
(905) 575-8800

Owner and chef Pat Delle Grazie is serious about cheese. And when you're famous for a stuffed pizza boasting almost *two pounds* of the highest-quality mozzarella, you gotta have lots on hand! Pat's menu is a veritable treasure trove of Italian dishes, including Chicken Red and White, which reminds John of his childhood. Unsurprisingly, everything on Pat's dessert menu—from cheese-

cakes to tiramisu—also contains cheese. You can understand why Pat doesn't bother counting how much cheese he goes through.

Culantro
Est. 2013
537 Main St. E
Hamilton, ON, L8M 1H9
(905) 777-0060
www.culantro.ca

You don't have to climb Machu Picchu to experience Peru's contribution to world wonders! Just head to Hamilton's Culantro, where chef Juan Castillo is serving up old family recipes loaded with Peruvian delights, like amarillo peppers and purple corn, which the Incans boiled down and drank. Rumour has it the purple corn has tremendous healing properties, but most people consume it for the taste. Juan serves this butterscotch-flavoured staple over crisp empanadas. You'll be inspired to book passage to Peru in no time!

The Harbour Diner
Est. 2008
486 James St. N
Hamilton, ON L8L 1J1
(905) 523-7373
www.harbourdiner.com

Most chefs have the luxury of spacious kitchens, but guys like Chris Preston are the true magicians, casting culinary spells in places without elbow room. Just how small is the Harbour's kitchen? Ask *You Gotta Eat Here*'s sound guy Scott. He stood in the back alley during the shoot. Nothing stops Chris from whipping up big meals with big taste, like crab and lobster macaroni and classic meatloaf. This is Mom's home cooking ratcheted up four notches. Join the lineup! At least you're not in the alley. Sorry, Scott!

Jack & Lois
Est. 2012
301 James St. N
Hamilton, ON L8R 2L4
(289) 389-5647
www.jackandlois.com

Calling all sandwich connoisseurs! If you love a good sammy, you're gonna line up for this place. They serve up everything you can place between a bun—from the Chancellor (chicken Parm like you've never seen) to a burger named after legendary Canadian comedian actor John Candy, which is topped with Canadian bacon and maple strip bacon and served on a glazed kaiser. With mismatched antique chairs and tables, chandeliers, and damask wallpaper, the space feels eclectic, retro, and totally laid back. A record player inviting customers to bring in their favourite albums only adds to the diner's charm.

The Ship
Est. 2009
23 Augusta St.
Hamilton, ON L8N 1P2
(905) 526-0792
www.theship.ca

From ship to shore, Hamilton's Ship has the best of land and sea onboard, with fresh seafood, sandwiches, and over-the-top burgers. Trey Leezer's the man steering this vessel through flavourful waters with dishes like his fried perch tacos served with a fresh and bright pico de gallo, homemade guac, and in-house coleslaw. You'll find The Ship docked on Hamilton's busy Augusta Street: an up-and-coming neighbourhood with tons of restaurants and bars. Anchors aweigh!

Pineapple Empanada (Culantro)

Perch BLT (The Ship)

LOCAL GEMS

City of Waterfalls

Hamilton is part of the Niagara Escarpment, which is so much more than its namesake landmark, Niagara Falls. In fact, the escarpment is a UNESCO World Bioshere Reserve. Hamilton itself is home to over 130 different waterfalls, earning it the nickname "The City of Waterfalls." If you're looking for an adventure, see if you can visit them all. Maps of the various waterfall locations are available at visitor centres and online. www.waterfalls.hamilton.ca.

Roma Bakery Slab Bread Pizza

If you're looking for a very Hamilton experience, look no further than Roma Bakery's famous slab pizza. Despite its immense popularity in Hamilton and the surrounding area, it's still one of the city's best-kept secrets. The bread pizza is well known for being affordable and healthy: the original recipe contains no trans fats, meat, or dairy. It's even available for purchase at local grocery stores, including Fortinos, Sobeys, and Metro. 233 Barton St., Stoney Creek, ON, L8E 2K4. www.romabakery.ca/pizza.html.

Uli's Stairs

In 2007, an Austrian immigrant known as Uli completed a 305-step stone staircase connecting lower and upper Hamilton neighbourhoods. Uli's stairs are a true labour of love, built by hand with a variety of natural and manufactured stone and concrete, and using tree branches for handrails. The staircase also features handmade benches and in places is lined with flowers and garden planters. Delightful homemade signs are placed at important markers along the trek. 440 Mountain Brow Blvd., Hamilton, ON, L8T 1A8.

That Little Place by the Lights
Est. 2009
76 Main St. E
Huntsville, ON P1H 2C7
(705) 789-2536
www.thatlittleplacebythelights.ca

. . . .

Italian immigrants Loris and Annie Buttus's restaurant features the best damn lasagna John has ever eaten (and he asks Zia Felicetta for forgiveness!). Much of Annie's secret lies in her Bolognese sauce. And don't miss dessert. Loris once ran a gelateria near Venice; now he's churning out delicious frozen treats for the people of Huntsville. *Mamma mia!*

LOCAL GEM

Treetop Trekking

Whether you want to scale a tree or zip-line through a forest, Treetop Trekking is the place to be in Ontario. Started in Quebec, the business has branched out to include five locations across Ontario, including one in Huntsville. Climb through obstacle courses, swing from tree to tree, navigate across balance logs, and traverse through rope bridges in a three-hour forest adventure. Treetop Trekking is open for its regular season from early April to mid-October, but is still available year-round for large groups. 1180 Highway 60, Huntsville, ON, P1H 1A3. www.treetoptrekking.com /en/huntsville.

KAWARTHA LAKES, ON, AND SURROUNDING AREA

The Riverside Inn Restaurant
Est. 2011
7497 Highway 35
Norland, ON K0M2L0
(705) 454-1045
www.riverside-inn.ca

At the Riverside Inn, everybody knows your name . . . and your order! Here regulars enjoy huge portions of diverse foods from po' boy wraps to comfort classics like French onion soup. Open year-round, this homey restaurant is a Kawartha community staple. In the winter, snowmobilers and locals come in for a bowlful of soup made from scratch and a skate around the homemade rink that owner James Burton builds out back. Hot chocolate is free for all!

LOCAL GEM
Kawartha Dairy

Best known for its wide variety of ice-cream flavours, Kawartha Dairy also sells milk, butter, and cream. In operation since 1937, Kawartha Dairy is definitely one of the crown jewels of the Kawartha Lakes and the area's most popular brand. Stop by most any grocery store or ice-cream parlour and you'll be sure to find Kawartha Dairy products for sale. (See www .kawarthadairy.com/where-to-buy for locations in Ontario.)

Dianne's
Est. 2013
195 Ontario St.
Kingston, ON K7L 2Y7
(613) 507-3474
www.dianneskingston.com

With no seafood place to call its own, Kingston went overboard for Dianne's, a Down East seafood shack meets Baja Mexico joint right on the water. Want crispy fish tacos? They've got 'em. Seafood-laden poutine? Mexican street corn, rustic salsa, and tequila shrimp? They've got those, too. Nestled by the water in a bright nautical-inspired space, Dianne's serves up flavours that have diners returning again, and again, and again. Seafood *olé*!

Geneva Crêpe Bistro
Est. 2010
297 Princess St.
Kingston, ON K7L 1B4
(613) 507-0297
www.genevacrepecafe.com

Pierre Elliot Trudeau's pastry chef taught Genevieve Patenaude to make crêpes back in the '70s, and people have been falling in love with hers ever since! With over forty delicious varieties, there's a crêpe to cater to every Canadian, including the prime minister! Try the Bombay, which overflows with smoked curry chicken, cranberries, coconut, almonds, and apples. Or for dessert, the Elvis is just the thing. You'll be shaking your hips to the tune of peanut butter, bananas, chocolate ganache, whipped cream, and smoked bacon! Yum.

Harper's Burger Bar

The Elvis (Geneva Crêpe Bistro)

Lasagna Grilled Cheese (MLTDWN)

Harper's Burger Bar
Est. 2010
93 Princess St.
Kingston, ON K7L 1A6
(613) 507-3663
www.harpersburgerbar.com

· · · · · · · · · · · · · · · · ·

Find your perfect burger match at Harper's Burger Bar, a hopping downtown Kingston joint that's sure to have just what you're craving. Chef Craig MacLennen has whipped up a menu of over twenty burger creations, like the adventurous Umani, topped with soya-glazed mushrooms and white truffle aioli. Craig says the restaurant needs to order 350 to 500 pounds of beef a week to keep up with demand! Harper's is a boisterous and high-energy place to socialize and unwind after a long day.

MLTDWN
Est. 2012
292 Princess St.
Kingston, ON K7L 1B5
(613) 766-1881
www.mltdwn.com

· · · · · · · · · · · · · · · ·

When Rahim and Aly Moloo dream, they dream in cheese! At MLTDWN, the brothers cook up fantastic grilled cheese. With so many wonderfully different creations on the menu, from out-of-this-world savoury to sinfully sweet, grilled cheese will never look—or taste—the same. For dessert, Rahim thinks outside the block, turning to cheese's sweet relative for inspiration. He grills cold cheesecake and graham cracker crumbs between two pieces of sweet crème brûlée French toast. Yes, please!

LOCAL GEMS

Look for Ghosts

Kingston was named the capital of Canada before Ottawa and has a long, storied history. And with history comes ghost stories. The Haunted Walk of Kingston has been operating for twenty years, and their cloaked, lantern-toting guides are a familiar sight after dark from spring until fall. Visit some of Kingston's most haunted sites on a variety of themed tours. The Haunted Walk also runs tours out of Ottawa and Toronto! www.hauntedwalk.com.

Go to Prison

Kingston is known for a lot of things, from its historic fort to the ivy-coated walls of Queen's University, but it's also the birthplace of the Correctional Services of Canada. Kingston celebrates this with pride by offering two unique prison tour experiences: one at the Kingston Penitentiary, which takes you through a guided tour of the now-closed maximum security prison, and the other just across the street at Canada's penitentiary museum, which shows you what prison was really like in an engaging eight-room display. 560 King St. W., Kingston, ON, K7L 4V7. www.kingstonpentour.com.

On the Road . . .
Again!

I love my job.

I mean, really. What could possibly be better? I *eat* for a living! Not only that, I get to visit amazing places and interact with the kindest, most passionate people you'll ever meet. Yet for all the benefits that come along with hosting *You Gotta Eat Here!*, there's one major challenge: the travel schedule.

A typical season of the show comprises seventy-eight restaurants, each of which requires two days of shooting, or 156 days in total. Add to that a minimum of fifty travel days (some of which can be really long since we're often in out-of-the-way places) and almost as many down days on the road and you can see that we're on the road *a lot*.

Don't get me wrong: I'm not complaining about how much we work. I know there are lots of people out there who work a lot more than we do. But being away from home and family for almost three-quarters of a year ain't easy, either. And that goes for those of us on the show and our partners at home, too.

I give a ton of credit to my amazing wife, who shoulders the burden of caring for our two daughters while I'm away. Even once I get home there's an adjustment phase. I'll admit I'm not particularly good at it (though I am getting better . . . right, honey?), but things go much more smoothly when I fit into *their* daily rhythm rather than trying to make them fit into *mine*.

It doesn't help that I'm often exhausted. Luckily, my house (and especially my couch!) is my recharge station, and the girls in my life understand that sometimes I just need to . . . well . . . lie there. Luckily the "couch phase" doesn't last very long and I'm soon back in the swing of things.

I think the great irony in all this is that once upon a time, I actually had a day job. I ended up quitting because I wanted to be a comedian, but also because I hated the idea of shaving every day. Now I carry the most elaborate shaving kit I could ever imagine, to make sure my face looks spotless every day we shoot.

And you know what? I love every minute of it. Just don't be surprised if you see me sporting a beard when I'm home.

By the looks of things, we haven't shot in a couple of days. Wait, I'm Italian! I sneeze and grow hair.

Jane Bond
Est. 1995
5 Princess St.
Waterloo, ON N2J 2H5
(519) 886-1689
www.janebond.ca

Jane Bond isn't a person, it's a state of mind, man. This restaurant is a throwback to California's '60s psychedelic culture, with crazy colours and a fun, laid-back atmosphere. Jane Bond's food is so filling it takes some customers a year to realize there's no meat on the menu. Serving hearty vegetarian fare like the Whoppie Burger and the Coconut and Peanut Curry, owner Josh Koehler and his family are expanding the minds and taste buds of the local academia.

The Lancaster Smokehouse
Est. 2011
574 Lancaster St. W
Kitchener, ON N2K 1M3
(519) 743-4331
www.lancsmokehouse.com

After fifteen years on the competitive barbecue circuit, passionate pit master Chris Corrigan brought the best eating from below the Mason-Dixon line home to Waterloo. Try the local specialties, like sweet and smoky pigtails made with a Southern spin, or Southern classics like oyster po' boys and spicy fried chicken at this family joint. Delicious eats, plus the restaurant's location in the historic Lancaster Tavern (est. 1840), make this business a local gem. Pull up a chair and dive in.

Taco Farm
Est. 2013
8 Erb St. W
Waterloo, ON N2L 1S7
(519) 208-1300
www.tacofarm.ca

If tacos grew on trees, we wouldn't need Taco Farm! Chef Nick Benninger makes tacos from scratch, pressing tortillas; brining, stewing, and smoking his meats; and concocting all manner of sauces—salsa, pesto, and pico. It's hard work, but it's a labour of love at Taco Farm. Tacos may be trendy, but Nick tries to make Taco Farm a family-friendly place. Decorated with graffiti and lots of natural wood, the spacious restaurant can handle its share of rowdy kids *and* babies.

LOCAL GEM

St. Jacob's Market

Wake up with the roosters and head over to Canada's largest year-round farmers' market. With hundreds of vendors, fresh fruit, vegetables, crafts, and delicious eateries, St. Jacob's is sure to please. Take a stroll through the various buildings to find the perfect homemade gift or just browse through the fresh produce and take it all in. Whatever you do, enjoy the bustling atmosphere and give yourself the opportunity to learn something new from one of the many vendors whose knowledge of their products has no bounds. 878 Weber St. N., Woolwich, ON, N2J 4A9. www.stjacobs.com/Farmers-Market-General-Information.htm.

LONDON, ON

The Bungalow
Est. 2009
910 Waterloo St.
London, ON N6A 3W9
(519) 434-8797
www.bungalowhub.ca

It's a bungalow on the outside, and a classic burger joint on the inside! Chef Nick Patterson tempted John with the Black & Blue Burger, a Cajun-coated delight and just one of many outrageous burger options, but the menu doesn't stop there. Enjoy bacon-wrapped scallops, sirloin steak, and most everything in between. It's no surprise that the Bungalow is well known throughout London. If you happen to walk into someone's living room by mistake, just ask them for the Bungalow. They'll know where to send you.

The Early Bird
Est. 2012
355 Talbot St.
London, ON N6A 2R5
(519) 439-6483
www.theearlybird.ca

The Early Bird is as long on personality as it is on cuisine, thanks to brothers Justin and Gregg Wolfe's wacky twists on diner food. When they're not playing in their heavy-metal band, they're serving up massive delicious portions. Try the Ginger Beer–Battered Tofu, the Popper, or Egg McJustin, dishes that have catapulted this retro, funky restaurant into the *You Gotta Eat Here!* Hall of Fame. Rock on!

Prince Albert's Diner
Est. 1985
565 Richmond St.
London, ON N6A 3G2
(519) 432-2835

· · · · · · · · · · · ·

What if we combined two things everybody loves: peanut butter and burgers? That's crazy, right? Turns out it isn't so nuts. Just ask Bill Spigos and his sister Betsy Kouklakis, who run the restaurant their father, George, bought in 1996. The Wally Burger is their winning combination of peanut butter and beef

patty. John's new motto: It ain't a burger if it ain't got the butter! Not convinced? Try the aptly named You Gotta Eat This Burger!

LOCAL GEMS

Banting House

Banting House celebrates the life and career of Sir Frederick Banting, the Canadian scientist best known for the discovery of insulin. This two-floor museum, which operates out of his old home, highlights interesting facts about Banting, his discovery, and the history of diabetes. Featuring historical artifacts, unique multimedia collections, and an exhibit of famous and influential people who have lived with diabetes, this museum is perfect for anyone with an interest in medicine or history in general. 442 Adelaide St. N., London, ON, N6B 3H8. www.bantinghousenhsc.wordpress.com.

Heart of London Walkabout Tour

Enjoy a personalized tour through the city of London and its colourful history all from the comfort of your phone. Learn everything you need to know about London from narrator Deb Rogers. Using her own humorous anecdotes to bring you tales from throughout history, Deb will show you the best of London and its most famous monuments and moments in history. Experience London like never before, visiting locations, learning about historical events, and hearing the stories of prominent local figures. www.londontourism.ca/Things-To-Do/Family-and-Fun /Heart-Of-London-Walkabout-Tour.

MONTREAL, QC

Brit & Chips
Est. 2010
5536 chemin de la Côte-des-Neiges
Montreal, QC H3T 1Y8
(514) 737-9555
www.britandchips.com

At Brit & Chips, chef Robert Stutman cooks up British classics like beer-battered fish and chips, Scotch eggs, and sausage rolls. But that's not all he's got in store! Rob likes to spike his fish batters with off-the-wall ingredients: everything from sour cream and onion chips to smoked meat and pickles! In this restaurant decorated with fishing gear, nets, and photos of old English ports, you'll be well chuffed, whether you're a traditionalist or a little cheeky.

Burger Bar
Est. 2011
1465 rue Crescent
Montreal, QC H3G 2B2
(514) 903-5575
www.montrealburger.com

Burger Bar adds a little *je ne sais quoi* to your hamburger with Quebec-inspired twists. How do you frenchify a burger? With toppings like blue cheese, Brie, foie gras, and, yes, poutine—piled high on a brioche bun. Brian Paquette created Montreal Burger Week's 2013 champion: the Hangover, a gravy-soaked burger topped with a tower of french fries, cheese curds, bacon, and a fried egg. Hangover: cured. Food coma: guaranteed. *C'est un* burger to do Montreal proud!

Cacao 70
Est. 2011
2087 rue Sainte-Catherine O
Montreal, QC H3H 1M6
(514) 933-1688
www.cacao70.ca

Chocolate has been seducing humans for thousands of years. And if Easy Ying at Montreal's Cacao 70 chocolate bar has anything to do with it, the pure bliss of a bittersweet bite is going to lead his patrons astray for a long time to come. With a multitude of different types of chocolate on the menu, chocolate waffles, chocolate crêpes, chocolate fondues, and chocolate parfaits are only the tip of this choco-chunk iceberg. Yum!

Chez Claudette
Est. 1983
351 avenue Laurier E
Montreal, QC H2T 1G7
(514) 279-5173
www.restaurantchezclaudette.com

Poutine defines the heart, soul, and taste buds of Montreal. Owners and chefs Adel Bakry and Jo-Anne McNeil know this all too well. How popular is poutine at Chez Claudette? Well, they offer twenty-five different kinds and every week make 165 quarts of gravy from scratch and lovingly hand cut 1700 pounds of potatoes. Try the most popular dish: the Toute Garnie (All Dressed). Pass the poutine, *s'il vous plaît*.

Icehouse
Est. 2011
51 rue Roy E
Montreal, QC H2W 2S3
(514) 439-6691

At this *You Gotta Eat Here!* Fan Favourite, food gets dumped on your table, and the music *du jour* is rock 'n' roll. The devil-may-care personality of owner, chef, and native Texan Nick Hodge comes through best in the Bucket Service of Fried Chicken. Roll up your sleeves and dig in. Bucket service is also available for Dr. Pepper Pork Ribs and authentic Southern crawfish.

L'Avenue

Est. 1994

922 avenue du Mont-Royal E

Montreal, QC H2J 1X1

(514) 523-8780

www.restaurantlavenue.ca

Montreal may be known for its night life, but you've gotta get up pretty early in the morning if you want a table at the city's legendary brunch spot L'Avenue, owned by Johnny Ditomasso. Try one of his inventive combinations, like the Sucré-Salé-Croustillant (Sweet-Salty-Crispy), or take a trip to Over-the-Topville with the Crêpes Américaines avec Pommes Caramélisées et Cheddar. English pancakes meet Montreal ingenuity.

Léché Desserts

Est. 2012

640 rue de Courcelle

Montreal, QC H4C 3C5

(514) 805-5600

www.lechedesserts.com

From pineapple upside-down cake to lemon meringue pie, pastry chef Josie loves to reinvent classics with her over-the-top doughnut specials. Past specials have included the PB&J and the Chicken Pot Pie Doughnut Pocket. Located in a former leather luggage factory in St. Henri, the twenty-two-seat Léché features

large wood beams, exposed brick, high ceilings, and an open kitchen that allows customers to watch the magic happen. *Léché* means "licked." Josie's handmade doughnuts and savoury doughnut-dough delights have customers licking their fingers clean.

The Main Deli Steak House

Est. 1974

3864 boulevard Saint-Laurent

Montreal, QC H2W 1Y2

(514) 843-8126

www.maindelisteakhouse.com

If there was a winner-take-all battle royale in Montreal to determine who's got the best smoked meat, you can bet that Peter Varvaro's Main Deli Steak House would be among the combatants. You can't go wrong with the classic smoked meat sandwich or the potato verenekes. The weekly 500-plus orders prove this *maison du bifthèque* has mastered the rib-eye, and there's no going back to store-bought desserts after tasting chef Diane Bass's German chocolate cakes.

Pizzeria Napoletana
Est. 1948
189 rue Dante
Montreal, QC H2S 1K1
(514) 276-8226
www.napoletana.com

If the essence of good Italian food is deliciousness in simplicity, then the Girolamo family—owners and chefs at Pizzeria Napoletana—have the winning recipe. With forty-one pizza and thirty-four pasta options, there's something for everyone. The key is the tasty tomato sauce, which goes on just about everything. Another outstanding feature is the polpette, a recipe Linda learned from her mother and grandmother. Tradition makes this a special place. When customers tell you it's just like Mama used to make, they're not kidding!

Poutineville
Est. 2010
1365 rue Ontario E
Montreal, QC H2L 1S1
(514) 419-5444
www.poutineville.com

What makes Poutineville's poutine unique? Try any number of the tantalizing toppings from fried corn dogs to succulently seared filet mignon. But more than that, *you* are the master of your mastication masterpiece. So dress your fries any way your mood suits you with the best-quality ingredients in the poutine biz, guaranteed by owner and master chef Kosta Kariotakis. Switch, swap, and salivate over the 1.5 million combinations of fries, cheeses, proteins, vegetables, and sauces. Your plate's like a mood ring, only poutine!

Prohibition
5700 avenue de Monkland
Montreal, QC H4A 1E4
(514) 481-8466
www.prohibitionmontreal.com

Matt Rouleau and Nicky Fournier's cozy brunch spot serves up unique comfort food dishes drawing from many influences. They playfully named their restaurant Prohibition after struggling to get a liquor license. But no one feels like they're missing out. Chef Brandon Walsh deep-fries his French toast, adds poached eggs and fried chicken to his poutine, and even turns humble yogurt into a rich and dippable breakfast with poached eggs, sheep's feta, and homemade paprika oil. Boring breakfasts are prohibited at Prohibition!

Satay Brothers
Est. 2011
3721 rue Notre-Dame O
Montreal, QC H4C 1P8
(514) 933-3507

Southeast Asia's just a meal away at Satay Brothers. After years of selling satays and steamed buns with their mom, Kim, at Montreal's Atwater Market, Alex and Mat Winnicki decided to open their own tribute to Southeast Asian hawker markets, bustling spots for casual, flavourful street food. They've traded butter and cream for galangal and lemongrass. Be sure to check out the creamy coconut laksa, bánh mì sandwiches, and steamed buns containing hoisin-braised pork belly. *C'est magnifique!*

Schwartz's Deli
Est. 1928
3895 boulevard Saint-Laurent
Montreal, QC H2W 1X9
(514) 842-4813
www.schwartzsdeli.com

Schwartz's is the granddaddy of all smoked meat joints in the smoked meat capital of the world. Founded in 1928 by Jewish Romanian immigrant Reuben Schwartz, it still wows its customers with good food rather than fancy decor (a single white-tiled room). If you're lucky enough to find a free seat inside, sit, smile, talk, and chow down on the best combination of meat, bread, and mustard. Just don't take *too* long—other people are waiting for your spot!

LOCAL GEMS

Gibeau Orange Julep

Only in Montreal can you find a giant three-storey orange protruding into the skyline that can be seen from almost anywhere in the city. The Gibeau Orange Julep was founded in 1932 and features a mysterious signature orange drink that people just can't get enough of, despite not knowing exactly what it contains. Though the quirky building design and delicious drink are the main attractions, it also serves classic diner-style food. 7700 boulevard Décarie, Montreal, QC, H4P 2H4.

Habitat 67

Habitat 67 is another permanent structure that originated from Montreal's World's Fair Exposition in 1967. Designed by Moshe Safdie as his graduate thesis, the building complex was created to temporarily house workers coming to the fair from around the world. Once these workers left, the geometric oddity became a suburban-style housing project for middle-class families: 354 identical boxes are stacked to make 146 separate apartments. 2600 avenue Pierre-Dupuy, Montreal, QC, H3C 3R6. www.habitat67.com/en.

Montreal Biosphere

Originally built for a display in the 1967 World Fair's Exposition, this structure was improperly installed due to budget constraints. Because it would be a problem to remove, the city chose to make it a permanent piece of Montreal's landscape. In the years since, the dome has survived a fire and a brutal Canadian ice storm. It is now known as the Montreal Biosphere, a museum dedicated to raising public awareness of environmental issues affecting the world today. 160 chemin Tour-de-l'Isle, Montreal, QC, H3C 4G8. www.ec.gc.ca/biosphere.

Crêperie Catherine
Est. 1995
977 rue Labelle
Mont-Tremblant, QC J8E 2W5
(819) 681-4888
www.creperiecatherine.ca

. . . .

After hittin' the slopes at Mont-Tremblant, visit Crêperie Catherine, a charming independent spot in the village. Skiers and boarders line up to devour savoury crêpes with chef Catherine Schmuck's signature garlic and mustard béchamel sauce or a sweet and velvety sucre a la crème. The walls at this chalet are adorned with Catherine's 500-plus chef figurine collection. Crêperie Catherine is the coziest place to go after a day on the slopes! Warning: You might have to roll down the mountain afterwards.

LOCAL GEM

Skyline Luge

Think there's nothing to do in Mont-Tremblant when there's no snow? Why not take a ride on the 1.4-kilometre luge track and experience the thrill of the Olympic sport in a controlled environment? Open from May to October, this track uses a unique go-kart-type vehicle to propel you down the winding track. Each cart features its own braking and steering system that allows you to customize your ride to your own comfort level, whether it's blinding fast or a slow journey down to enjoy the scenery. 1000 chemin du Curé Deslauriers, Mont-Tremblant, QC, J8E 1E1. www.skylineluge.com/luge-canada/skyline-luge-mont-tremblant.

Barb's Country Kitchen
Est. 2013
634041 Highway 10
Orangeville, ON L9W2Z1
(519) 938-8282
. . . .

At Barb's Country Kitchen, married couple Barb and Angelo Stratigos are a team made in foodie heaven. A self-proclaimed big guy, Angelo's biggest fear is people leaving his restaurant hungry. With Barb's astronomical portions, that doesn't seem likely. Angelo comes up with crazy concepts like the Manwich Breakfast Sandwich or the Banana Bread French Toast, and she cooks 'em up. The *huge* portions have Orangeville welcoming Barb and Angelo with open arms and full tummies!

Barley Vine Rail Company
Est. 2013
35 Armstrong St.
Orangeville, ON L9W 3H6
(519) 942-3400
www.thebvrco.com
. . . .

Hop the train to the Barley Vine Rail Company, the perfect spot to get away from all the hullabaloo with a little homestyle cooking. The BVR makes its home in a refurbished train station—Orangeville's original hub for travel. At the helm is Jason Cooney, a big-city chef who's found his groove making stick-to-your-ribs dishes like perogies packed with creamy buttermilk mashed potatoes. All aboard!

Philadelphia Kitchen

Est. 2011
281 Broadway Ave.
Orangeville, ON L9W 1L2
(519) 938-8970
www.philadelphiakitchen.ca

When Philadelphia native Joe Lattari came to Canada, he encountered a problem: there wasn't an authentic Philly cheesesteak to be found for miles. Undaunted, Joe started making Philly classics for friends, who encouraged him to open up his own sandwich shop, following in his family's footsteps. Joe makes some of the most unbelievable cheesesteak *You Gotta Eat Here!* has ever tried, and there are plenty of non-traditional options, too. Call them simple if you dare, but to PK's thousands of devoted customers, these sandwiches are exquisite.

Soulyve

Est. 2009
34 Mill St.
Orangeville, ON L9W 2M3
(519) 307-5983
www.soulyve.ca

Who says good deeds go unnoticed? In 1996, to raise money for school-building initiatives in Jamaica, Philip Dewar and Joshua Blake sold homemade Jamaican classics at a farmers' market, and the response was overwhelming. When their catering business couldn't keep up with demand, the answer was Soulyve, where Caribbean "soul" food meets fresh, "live" ingredients. Rocking traditional Jamaican mainstays like ackee and salted codfish and curried goat, Philip and Josh keep doing their good deeds, one dish at a time.

LOCAL GEMS

Art Walk of Tree Sculptures

Orangeville is host to a unique art project that has transformed dead or dying trees into works of art. Scattered around the town, more than fifty wood carvings from over a dozen sculptors are just waiting to be seen. Visit the town hall or public library to pick up a brochure that includes a map of the sculpture locations, information on individual sculptors, and a brief history of the art walk project. www.orangevilletourism.ca/attractions/attraction/art-walk-of-tree-sculptures.

Glasscraft

Glasscraft offers a unique experience where you can browse through a large collection of glasswork items and learn how to make them yourself. Working from two locations (one in Orangeville and the other in nearby Grand Valley), artist Bill Adler can lead you in a beginner's course or help you hone your skills in glass art. Classes include bead making, glass fusing, mirror etching, mosaics, and much more. 159 Broadway, Orangeville, ON, L9W 1K2; 31 Main St., Grand Valley, ON, L0N 1G0. www.glasscraftcanada.ca.

Tre Sorelle
Est. 2004
133 Mississauga St. E
Orillia, ON L3V 5A9
(705) 325-8507
www.tresorelleorillia.com

. . . .

Take three hot-blooded Italian women, recipes that go back seven decades, and a dedication to homestyle meals and you've got Tre Sorelle (three sisters). Gina White, Lisa Partichelli, and Carla Paluzzi join forces with the rest of the family to create the most delicious lasagna. Here, everyone is part of *la famiglia*. So what if the sisters have the odd spat? That's just adds to Tre Sorelle's old-world charm.

LOCAL GEM
Mariposa Market Store
This quaint family-owned market features some of the best products Orillia has to offer. Featuring a café, bakeshop, candy store, home deco store, and selection of handmade aromatherapy items like soaps and candles, this turn-of-the-century building contains so many things to see. Take a seat at their feel-good food café or stroll through the stores. You can even put together your own gift basket to bring back to friends or family after your trip to this beautiful small-town gem. No matter what you do, Mariposa is sure to impress. 109 Mississauga St. E., Orillia, ON, L3V 1V6. www.mariposamarket.ca.

OTTAWA, ON

Art-Is-In Boulangerie
Est. 2006
250 City Centre Ave., #112
Ottawa, ON K1R 1C7
(613) 695-1226
www.artisinbakery.com

Art-Is-In Boulangerie started as *the* place to get Ottawa's best bread. Now it's *the* place to get chef and bread-head Kevin Mathieson's ultra-creative sandwiches! Classics like the BLT, meatball sub, and club sandwich have received the foie gras, duck confit, and pork belly treatment as much for fun as flavour. And then there's each bun, specially designed to maximize the experience. The flavours are changing all the time in this refurbished loading dock of a 1940s train station located downtown Ottawa. You gotta eat here!

Burgers 'n' Fries Forever
Est. 2013
329 Bank St.
Ottawa, ON K2P 1X9
(613) 230-3456
www.burgersnfriesforever.com

A burger without fries is like a yin without a yang—incomplete. Thankfully, at Burgers 'n' Fries Forever, both parts of the meal are highlighted with fun and delicious toppings like homemade guacamole, beef bacon, deep-fried jalapeños, and your choice of several house-made sauces. Chef and owner Jamil Bhuya hand-cuts over 1000 pounds of potatoes a week to make the European-style frites that inspire him. When you come to Burgers 'n' Fries Forever, you'll feel complete—completely full, that is!

El Camino
Est. 2013
380 Elgin St.
Ottawa, ON K2P 1N1
(613) 422-2800
www.eatelcamino.com

. . . .

At El Camino, owner Matthew Carmichael and chef Jordan Holley are doing up Asian street food–inspired tacos right. Using ingredients like Chinese cardamom, lime leaves, and achiote, Jordan turns the volume way up on everything from tuna tartare to ox tongue. At four bucks a taco, it's no wonder there's a lineup down the street! Every. Single. Day.

Elgin Street Diner
Est. 1993
374 Elgin St.
Ottawa, ON K2P 1N1
(613) 237-9700
www.elginstreetdiner.com

. . . .

The Elgin Street Dinner is an *institution* in the best sense of the word: it's open every minute of every day, doesn't have a lock on the door, and boasts down-the-street lineups at three in the morning. Owner and chef Ron Shrybman draws the crowds with his mouth-watering diner food, including the famous Blue Plate Breakfast, poutine, and chili. Put Elgin Street on your Taste Bud Map and visit anytime!

The Manx
Est. 1993
370 Elgin St.
Ottawa, ON K2P 1N1
(613) 231.2070
www.manxpub.com

. . . .

The Manx's black cat logo has perched, friendly and familiar, on the corner of Elgin and Frank streets for over twenty years now. This true Ottawa institution may look like a public house, but the pub grub made by big and burly chef Jarrah Thomas-Reynolds pounces on you with savoury surprises! Traditional shepherd's pie is reimagined as Moroccan Braised Short Ribs. The Manx's wildly diverse patrons are brilliantly reflected and deliciously served by this internationally inspired menu.

Art-Is-In Boulangerie

Bobotie (Stoneface Dolly's)

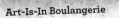

(Two Six {Ate})

Chef Steve Harris
(Two Six {Ate})

Pressed

Est. 2011
750 Gladstone Ave.
Ottawa, ON K1R 6X5
(613) 680-9294
www.pressed-ottawa.com

. . . .

Leave your laundry at home—the only thing being cleaned up here is the food. At Pressed, which occupies a sweet (or savoury) spot between fast food and fine dining, Jeff Stewart creates culinary harmony with hot griddles, bread, and batter. After quitting his job on Parliament Hill to pursue his passions in the kitchen, not the cubicle, Jeff never looked back. Now whether you choose the spicy jerk chicken sandwich or the Big Apple Waffle, you'll get food that's lick-your-plate-clean yummy.

The SmoQue Shack

Est. 2011
129 York St.
Ottawa, ON K1N 5T4
(613) 789-4245
www.smoqueshack.com

. . . .

No one loves barbecue as much as we do, and this is one of our favourite places to get it. Earthy, tantalizingly flavourful, and spicy without being too hot, the Shack's Jamaican jerk pork is a testament to chef Warren Sutherland's heritage and talent. Can't decide which meat to stuff in your face? Try a sample platter, a parade of slow-cooked Jamaican delights. At this *You Gotta Eat Here!* Fan Favourite, every dish is smoky, saucy, and Caribbean-y.

Stoneface Dolly's

Est. 1995
416 Preston St.
Ottawa, ON K1S 4M9
(613) 564-2222
www.stonefacedollys.com

. . . .

Stoneface Dolly's reputation for amazing food has spawned a following so devout they'll brave winter lineups for a spot at a table. Named after the original owner's mother, an exceptional poker player, the restaurant has everybody going all in for its French toast, made with homemade molasses bread. Thanks to owner Bob Russell's roots, there are also delicious South African dishes like the chicken (or tofu) bobotie (*buh-BOO-tee*), giving the dinner menu international flair. Play your cards right and visit!

Two Six {Ate}

Est. 2012
268 Preston St.
Ottawa, ON K1R 7R3
(613) 695-8200
www.twosixate.com

Two Six {Ate} is the perfect place in Ottawa to ruin your appetite. It's the grown-up version of your favourite after-school hangout, complete with lots of seating, a full range of snack food–inspired dishes, and even an arcade game. Zany chef Steve Harris happily serves up upgraded classic munchies like his chicken confit poutine and Not Your Mom's Velveeta. Regardless of whether you eat from the small plate or the full menu, you're guaranteed to be full by dinner!

makes everything in house with only the freshest ingredients. Try the Dagwood, a triple-decker sandwich; the Poutine Galvaude, fries topped with house-roasted chicken and peas; or the Eggs in Purgatory, a fireball of a dish.

Wilf & Ada's

Est. 2014 (formerly Ada's Diner 1994)
510 Bank St.
Ottawa, ON K2P 1Z4
(613) 231-7959
www.wilfandadas.com

Who says brunch is just for weekends? Not fans of Wilf & Ada's! This intimate restaurant serves brunch all day, every day. Dominic Paul's menu of signature French toast, Bennies, and homemade bacon keeps customers wishing there were more days in a week! Dom

LOCAL GEMS

Balanced Sculptures

You may wonder how these stacks of rocks keep themselves from falling over, but that's all part of their magic. Designed by John Ceprano and located on the shores of the Ottawa River, these sculptures symbolize harmony with nature. Each hand-built sculpture has been balanced and stabilized, but to protect them from damage, it's best to avoid touching them. Walk among the stacked rocks and explore the wonder of this unique art installation. Remic Rapids, Sir John A. Macdonald Parkway, Ottawa, ON. www.jfceprano.com/sculpture.

Mrs. Tiggy Winkle's

In operation since 1977, Mrs. Tiggy Winkle's is a true piece of Ottawa's entertainment history. With four locations across the city and a bustling online catalogue to boot, this is a can't-miss toy store for all. Toys, puzzles, games, books, and more line the walls of these quirky stores. The "Lost Marbles" section is also a crowd-pleaser, featuring vintage and retro toys. With Mrs. Tiggy Winkle's longstanding presence in the toy industry, its stores stock only the best and most interesting items to ensure you won't be let down. www.mrstiggywinkles.ca.

Pinhey's Point

The historic site of Pinhey's Point consists of a large home and 88 acres of parkland operated by the City of Ottawa. Well known to locals, this picturesque spot isn't a typical tourist destination, meaning you'll be more likely to enjoy some classic Ottawa culture here. The building—dubbed Horaceville after the Pinhey family's oldest son, Horace—was established in 1920. Tour the property and discover the history of the Pinhey family through artifacts, paintings, and more. 270 Pinhey's Point Rd., Dunrobin, ON, K0A 1T0. www.pinheyspoint.ca.

Scary, Scary, Scary
The Dark Side of
You Gotta Eat Here!

Psst. You.

Yeah, you. I know what you're thinking.

You think being a part of the *You Gotta Eat Here!* team is a cushy job. You think we never have to face danger, or action, or even the undead. Well, I'm here to say that you're wrong. You see, along the way, the crew and I have had our fair share of run-ins with danger. And I'm happy to report we survived them all.

Want ghosts? During five years of shooting, we've stayed in a few scary hotels, but none compares with the Pontchartrain Hotel in New Orleans, which is said to be haunted by as many as twenty-five spirits (that is *not* a typo, people). We didn't know about the Pontchartrain's colourful history before we got there, but we clued in quickly enough when we got off the plane and told our van driver where we were going, only to have him respond, "Ohhh no!" Turns out he had worked at the Pontchartrain some years before but only lasted two weeks because he was too creeped out by the "other" guests.

I didn't have any other-worldly experiences during our stay (other than a floating plate of beignets in my room, that is), but director Jim Morrison wasn't so lucky. Jim was convinced something had visited his room in the night after he woke up one morning to find that a drawer—which was shut tight when he went to bed—was wide open the next morning. To this day, he swears he never touched it.

Want near misses? We've got those, too. Back in 2012, we were driving from Toronto to Windsor, Ontario, with Josh behind the wheel, Jim in the passenger seat, and me in the back listening to the Italy-Ireland soccer match on my headphones. Here's how the chain of events unfolded:

- Italy scores
- Italian guy in back seat screams uncontrollably, just as we're passing a tractor-trailer
- Guys in front think guy in back is screaming because adjacent tractor-trailer is moving into their lane and is about to kill them all
- Guys in front start screaming uncontrollably
- Guy in back seat laughs uncontrollably at screaming guys in front seat
- Nobody dies, though a few throats are ever-so-slightly damaged in the process

What, not close enough for you? Well, there was also the time we were flying into Toronto from Montreal with a wicked crosswind. Seems the pilot thought it would be cool to land on only one back wheel and drive down the runway like that for a while, only to realize he or she (I never checked) had run out of tarmac to put the plane down for real. So we had to pull up at the last second, do a big loop around the city, then land again.

Nobody got hurt then, either. Well, except the guy sitting next to me, who apparently still has my fingernail marks buried in the flesh of his left forearm.

PETERBOROUGH, ON

Reggie's Hot Grill

Est. 2007
89 Hunter St. E
Peterborough, ON K9H 1G4
(705) 874-1471
www.reggieshotgrill.ca

. . . .

In 2009, best buds Reggie Maranda and Cam Green's wildly success-ful chip truck morphed into a year-round burger joint. They played a friendly game of darts to determine the name. Guess who won? The customers! One fave is the Big Boppa Burger. With its hand-crafted cream cheese and spinach sauce sandwiched between two patties, it's like a cream-filled doughnut . . . of meat. Here, good karma is grilled up daily—even Hawaiian style.

Two Dishes Cookshop

Est. 2014
261 Charlotte St.
Peterborough, ON K9J 2V3
(705) 775-2650
www.twodishescookshop.tumblr.com

. . . .

Thanks to its big ol' rooster painted on the front, it's hard to miss downtown Peterborough's comfort food hot spot, owned by sisters Susan and Paula Houde. The menu is inspired by seasonal local ingre-dients. From the bread and biscuits to ketchup and cola, everything on your table is made the Cookshop way: from scratch. Susan makes classics you know like chicken and biscuits, and introduces you to new favourites like the Smoked Trout Pancake. Pull up a chair!

LOCAL GEM

Canadian Canoe Museum

Once one of the most common methods of transportation in Canada, canoes have a long history from coast to coast. Celebrate this history at the Canadian Canoe Museum, which features over 100 canoes, kayaks, and other types of paddled watercrafts. The collection spans the country, with dugout canoes from the First Nations of the Pacific Northwest to Newfoundland's Beothuk bark canoes and a everything in between. Educational opportunities abound at this distinctive historic museum. 910 Monaghan Rd., Peterborough, ON, K9J 5K4. www.canoemuseum.ca.

PeterboRoutes

The City of Peterborough has worked hard to build its reputation as a premier biking location in Ontario. PeterboRoutes offers a mix of city and country trails, providing cycling enthusiasts with some spectacular options in and around Peterborough. Explore the area at your own pace with eight different plotted trails to choose from, all featuring unique paths and different levels of difficulty. A noteworthy mention is the uphill battle that is the Tour du Tarts, which takes you from one award-winning butter tart location to another. www.peterborough.ca/Assets/City+Assets/LIS /Documents/Cycling+Route+Map.pdf.

Casa Calzone
Est. 2000
1298 rue de la Pointe-aux-Lièvres
Quebec City, QC G1L 4L9
(418) 522-3000
www.casacalzone.com

Joe Gamper is seriously passionate about calzones. He's been involved in the family restaurant since he was thirteen, and now he runs the business opened by their dad, Horst. At Casa Calzone, you can expect Joe's amazing calzones to be bursting with any of the following fillings: crispy sausage, creamy goat cheese, gooey Brie, spicy red jalapeños—and, oh yeah, it might be on fire, too! Don't worry. A fire extinguisher is always on hand, and so are delicious flavours.

Le Chic Shack
Est. 2012
15 rue du Fort
Quebec City, QC G1R 3W9
(418) 692-1485
www.lechicshack.ca

Owned by Lucy and Evan Price, Le Chic Shack in Québec City is breaking new ground in the birthplace of poutine and daring to shake things up! Chef Mikael Garneau ladles gravy on the bottom, smashes potatoes instead of chipping them, and uses bold toppings like crème fraîche and bordelaise sauce. Try La Braisée or La Fumée, made with salty Montreal smoked meat. It's a Montreal classic presented in a revolutionary way. *Sacré bleu!*

LOCAL GEMS

Fun on the Funicular

The Old Quebec Funicular was built in 1879 as a means to connect the Lower Town (Basse-Ville) and Upper Town (Haute-Ville) of Quebec City. Before it existed it took quite a hike to get from one part of town to another. A fellow by the name of William Griffith decided to fix the problem. At 64 metres in length, the funicular travels on a 45-degree angle and deposits you 59 metres above its starting point at the historic House Louis Jolliet. Funiculaire du Vieux-Québec Inc., 16 Petit-Champlain, Quebec, QC, G1K 4H4. www.funiculaire-quebec.com.

SAULT STE. MARIE, ON

Ernie's Coffee Shop
Est. 1950
13 Queen St. E
Sault Ste. Marie, ON P6A 1Y4
(705) 253-9216

Since 1950, the Febbraro family has served the Soo three meals a day in this cozy diner where jukebox music plays and friendly waiters work the tables. Don't be fooled by the restaurant's name, cuz coffee ain't all they got! Enjoy home-cooked meals like their traditional chicken Parmesan, and be sure to order dessert ahead of time to be guaranteed a slice of Chuck's famous coconut cream pie. This busy spot boasts some serious nostalgia for everyone in town.

Low & Slow
Est. 2014
480 Albert St. W
Sault Ste. Marie, ON P6A 1C3
(705) 450-6328
www.eatlownslow.com

Low & Slow may be up in Sault Ste. Marie, but don't be fooled! This blue-collar barbecue fusion joint owned by Chad Stewart, Jen Richards, and Blake Richards looks, feels, and tastes like it belongs down South. Whether it's wet or dry ribs, brisket with a secret house rub, or smoked ham, sausage, or turkey, they use their smoker to low and slow cook everything. And it's not just meat in these smokers. They even use them for oven-smoked chocolate cheesecake!

August Restaurant
Est. 2008
5204 King St.
Beamsville, ON L0R 1B3
(905) 563-0200
www.augustrestaurant.ca

If it's comfort food you crave, head out to August, where chef and owner Beth Ashton cooks up heart-warming classics full of cream and butter for Beamsville brunchers. Diners rave about Beth's cinnamon bun French toast with candied pecans, over-sized sandwiches, Benedicts, and savoury pastries. It's food you'll jump out of bed for as soon as the rooster crows. August is bright and cheery, clad in green and purple walls and furnished with wood tables and wrought-iron chairs. It's like an indoor backyard party!

The Bull BBQ Pit
Est. 2011
24 St. Paul St.
St. Catharines, ON L2R 3M2
(905) 397-3287
www.thebullbbqpit.com

At the Bull BBQ Pit, Omar Fawzy whips up inventive renditions of kid classics and old-school barbecue favourites and gives them wacky names, including the Redonkadonk and the Frick & Frack. He draws on thirty years of family-style restaurant experience to create unmatched dishes. Attracting everyone from college students scarfing down the mac 'n' cheese–loaded Cheezy Weezy to locals devouring the smoky and zingy Philly Cheese Steak, the Bull is St. Catharines' place to be!

The Garrison House
Est. 2012
111C Garrison Village Dr., #2
Niagara-on-the-Lake, ON L0S 1J0
(905) 468-4000
www.thegarrisonhouse.ca

Joe Feta's Greek Village
Est. 1995
290 Lake St.
St. Catharines, ON L2N 4H5
(905) 646-3399
www.joefetas.ca

Garrison House is a local pub with food that's anything but ordinary. Owners David Watt and Leigh Atherton wanted the restaurant to be a meeting place for neighbours to hang out and eat great food together. David knows his customers by name (and, of course, their favourite dish). His hearty pub food is all about English classics, which get an upgrade with David's use of a little fat, a little beer, and a whole lot of tender loving care! However, they have also branched out beyond England's border to offer a curry dish and a vegan pho noodle bowl.

The philosophy of Greek restaurants is "the more, the merrier." Well, at Joe Feta's, with every extra parent, sibling, uncle, or cousin who joins the party, there's more love and more laughs to go around. Now run by George Kountourogiannis and his family, Joe Feta's is a landmark famous for its mainstay: souvlaki. Uncle Angelo prepares up to 300 every day! And don't miss the saganaki, fried goat cheese set aflame right at your table! It'll grab your taste buds and everyone's attention. *Opa!*

Niagara's Welland Canal

Explore Niagara's Welland Canal system with its numerous locks and bridges. Spanning 11 kilometres along the Niagara Peninsula and featuring four swing lift bridges and three vertical lift bridges, the system offers a unique experience— whether you're in a boat or on dry land. You can watch cargo ships and pleasure crafts cruise through the eight locks from viewing platforms located along the system, and experience activities and learning opportunities in each of the four towns that it connects: Thorold, St. Catharines, Welland, and Port Colborne. www.niagarawellandcanal.com.

LOCAL GEMS

Lakeside Park Carousel

Take your kids for a ride and experience a blast from the past with a classic carnival ride. Featuring sixty-eight hand-carved animals, including horses, camels, giraffes, lions, and goats, as well as music played from an antique organ, this carousel is sure to bring out the kid in everyone. Sticking to its original pricing at only five cents a ride, this carousel, built between 1898 and 1905, is a piece of history that never gets old. Lakeside Park, 1 Lakeport Rd., St. Catharines, ON, L2N 5B3. www.stcatharines.ca/en/experiencein/lakesideparkcarousel.asp.

Morningstar Mill

Experience the old days of flour-making at Morningstar Mill, a working grist mill and heritage site that was in operation between 1883 and 1933. The mill was built in 1872, along with a turbine shed, a blacksmith and carpentry shop, a saw mill, and the home of the Morningstar family (restored to its 1933 appearance). The mill still uses all of the original equipment and techniques of the late 19th and early 20th centuries to grind grain into flour. 2714 Decew Rd., St. Catharines, ON, L0S 1E6. www.morningstarmill.ca.

STRATFORD, ON

Boomers Gourmet Fries
Est. 1998
26 Erie St.
Stratford, ON N5A 1B2
(519) 275-3147
www.boomersgourmetfries.com

. . . .

Boomers' cantankerous yet lovable owner and chef Sue Pasquale has a unique perspective on deep-fried Yukon Gold potatoes and on life. At this tiny fry-and-burger joint, you can feast on twelve combinations of fries and gravy, plus a slew of delicious burgers (including the S.O.B., named after Sue herself!). Boomers patrons eat what Sue tells them to. Who wants to argue with a woman who tosses a 50-pound sack of potatoes over her shoulder like it's a baby?

LOCAL GEM

Savour Stratford Trails

Stratford offers unique "trail" experiences, including the Savour Stratford Chocolate Trail, the Savour Stratford Bacon and Ale Trail, and additional seasonal trails throughout the year. These routes allow visitors to check out numerous locations across the city to taste test the best Stratford has to offer. Each trail varies in price between $25 and $30, but all will leave your taste buds satisfied. Explore the city through food and discuss what you eat with the culinary stars of Stratford. www.visitstratford.ca

THUNDER BAY, ON

Hoito Restaurant
Est. 1918
314 Bay St.
Thunder Bay, ON P7B 1S1
(807) 345-6323
www.thehoito.ca

. . . .

The nearly 100-year-old Hoito is one of our youthful country's most storied restaurants. It was originally located in the Finnish Labour Temple's basement and run as a co-operative, largely for local Finnish-Canadian bushworkers who finished their long, hard days with monstrous appetites. The Hoito, whose name means "care," provided large portions at low prices while still maintaining communal ownership for everyone who ate there. Customers today still feel the love, flocking here for the legendary Finnish pancakes and Karelian pasties, even in a bone-chilling Thunder Bay winter!

LOCAL GEM

The Persian Man

Thunder Bay is known for many things, but ask any local what the delicacy of the city is and they'll most likely tell you it's a Persian. Offered at only one location in the entire country—the Persian Man—this cinnamon bun–like sweet roll is coated in a layer of either raspberry- or strawberry-flavoured icing (there is intense debate among locals to describe the actual flavour) and is considered a must-have for any visitor to Thunder Bay. 899 Tungsten St., Thunder Bay, ON, P7B 6H2.

TORONTO, ON

5 Doors North
Est. 1997
2088 Yonge St.
Toronto, ON M4S 2A3
(416) 480-6234
www.fivedoorsnorth.com

. . . .

Chef Vito Rizzuto has been serving homemade gnocchi in Gorgonzola sauce for seventeen years at this Toronto institution. His customers won't let him change a thing! Another specialty is the BBQ baby back ribs, a simply delicious meat-and-potatoes dish. The

5 Doors' most coveted dessert is the chocolate banana bread pudding. Many 5 Doors regulars have grown up with Vito's homey cooking and bring their families back every week.

Banh Mi Boys
Est. 2011
392 Queen St. W
Toronto, ON M5V 2A6
(416) 363-0588
www.banhmiboys.com

. . . .

A family Viet-sub business, Banh Mi Boys go for gold with top-notch, pan-Asian takes on bánh mì sandwiches, steamed buns, and Asian tacos. Their food has won them loyal worshippers, who come for fresh, bright ingredients, light, crusty loaves, and meticulously prepared fillings. They're lined up down the block! You gotta eat here!

Barque Smokehouse

Est. 2011

299 Roncesvalles Ave.

Toronto, ON M6R 2M3

(416) 532-7700

www.barque.ca

. . . .

When David Neinstein and Jonathan Persofsky tired of corporate life, they decided to open a smokehouse specializing in brunches. Barque now has one of the fastest-growing followings in Toronto. Try the daring Barque Benedict or the melt-in-your-mouth 12-Hour-Brisket. Who knows? Maybe your visit will inspire you to quit your job, too!

Beast

Est. 2010

96 Tecumseth St.

Toronto, ON M6J 2H1

(647) 352-6000

www.thebeastrestaurant.com

. . . .

Unleash your beast! From the Beast Burger to a bacon-topped doughnut that customers phone ahead for, there are plenty of brunch dishes to devour at Beast. When Scott Vivian and Rachelle Cadwell took over the restaurant space on Tecumseth Street, they set out to create a neighbourhood hub with a homey feel. They live in the apartment upstairs, so it's home to them as well as their customers. Pull up a chair!

The Borough

Est. 2014

1352 Danforth Ave.

Toronto, ON M4J 1M9

(416) 901-1429

www.borough.ca

. . . .

No need to cross the pond. Head to the Borough for the best taste of Jolly Old England in Toronto. Anglophile Jason Ashworth's got all of your favourites: Yorkshire puddings, meat pies, and bangers and mash. The Borough's become a local hot spot for Toronto East Enders who come for the deliciously simple food and cozy atmosphere. With some sweet and sticky toffee pudding for dessert, you'll be singing "Rule Britannia"!

The Burger's Priest

Est. 2010
3397 Yonge St.
Toronto, ON M4N 2M7
(416) 488-3510
www.theburgerspriest.com

Meet owner Shant Mardirosian, a seminary dropout and true believer whose new calling is to redeem the lowly hamburger and help it claim its rightful place in the next world. He's converting thousands every week at Burger's Priest through his secret menu, where religious puns flow as freely as the french fries. Ask for the Religious Hypocrite, the Holy Smokes, or the Red Sea. Bow down your head and worship, burger lover. The service is about to start, and the Priest is in the house.

Café Polonez

Est. 1978
195 Roncesvalles Ave.
Toronto, ON M6R 2L5
(416) 532-8432
www.cafepolonez.ca

Offering the most authentic and delicious homemade Polish food money can buy since 1978, Café Polonez is unique. Its Beet Root Soup with Dumplings and chef Danusia Olesinska's four varieties of homemade perogies are just the beginning of the European hit parade at Café Polonez, whose menu includes everything from herring to ground meat cutlets, hunter's stew to Polish sausage. Another fave is chef Marcin Molek's traditional crêpes! A dedication to fresh, delicious, homemade food makes Café Polonez a mainstay in an ever-changing culinary landscape.

Cardinal Rule

Est. 2011
5 Roncesvalles Ave.
Toronto, ON M6R 2K2
(647) 352-0202
www.cardinalrulerestaurant.com

Cardinal Rule owners Katie James and Marta Kusel take traditional homestyle diner food and flip it on its behind. Try their Maki 'n' Cheese, where a classic transforms into sushi, or their meat muffins, a twist on meatloaf. For brunch, feast on the Hail Caesar Eggs Benedict if you're the type who likes to wash down your eggs with a Caesar. Chilled, groovy, traditional, and modern all in one, Cardinal Rule sits dangerously close to the top of our must-eat list.

Caplansky's

Est. 2009
356 College St.
Toronto, ON M5T 1S6
(416) 500-3852
www.caplanskys.com

Caplansky's has become a household name in Toronto. Chef Zane

Caplansky spent five years perfecting his smoked meat recipe before opening for business in a small room in the Monarch Tavern, eventually moving to the full-service resto on College Street. In addition to delectable sandwiches, brisket, signature latkes, and mouth-watering slaw, you gotta try a Fat Sam's Grand Slam, featuring all of Caplansky's deli meats piled onto double rye. Caplansky's is growing fast, with locations now open in Yorkville and Terminals 1 and 3 in Toronto's Pearson International Airport.

Casa Manila
Est. 2010
879 York Mills Rd.
Toronto, ON M3B 1Y5
(416) 443-9654
www.casamanila.ca

. . . .

With a cuisine influenced by Spanish, Asian, and Latin flavours, Filipinos were doing "fusion" way before it was cool—and you can experience it without leaving the GTA! Sample chef and owner Mila Nabor Cuachon's delicious menu through Casa Manila's kamayan party experience. Order ahead and arrive to a table covered in banana leaves and courses served family-style with no plates or cutlery. Even if you've never tasted savoury peanut Kare Kare Beef Stew, you'll feel at home at Casa Manila.

Chino Locos
Est. 2008
4 Greenwood Ave.
Toronto, ON M4L 2P4
(647) 345-5626
www.chinolocos.com

. . . .

We love burritos *and* Chinese food. Luckily for us, Chino Locos combines the best of both worlds. It's the product of Minh La and Victor Su's intense collective desire to give Torontonians hip-hop cool food for a reasonable price. Try the Slow Roast Pork Burrito or Da Finest Fish Burrito. Sure, there are red-and-white checkered floors, but you're more likely to hear Jay-Z than Fats Domino. That's if you can hear anything over the sound of food being stuffed into your mouth.

The Clubhouse Sandwich Shop
Est. 2013
455 Spadina Ave.
Toronto, ON M5S 2G8
(647) 502-1291

. . . .

You won't need a password to get into the Clubhouse, a thriving Toronto sandwich shop catering to Toronto's student community. You'll be happy to take a study break with chef Doan Nguyen's outside-the-box sandwiches, which get top marks. Where else can you find full pork chops or deep-fried turkey thighs between two buns? Fuel your brain with Doan's flank steak

The Beastwich (The Beast)

Rachelle Cadwell and Scott Vivian
(The Beast)

Tequila Smoked Chicken with
Rootbeer Beans (Hogtown Smoke)

A dog to die for (Fancy Franks)

sandwich or smoked chicken sandwich. With sauces and toppings to match, the Clubhouse is the best club on or off campus!

The Combine Eatery
Est. 2011
162 Danforth Ave.
Toronto, ON M4K 1N2
(416) 792-8088
www.thecombineeatery.com

You don't have to go south of the border to get incredible Southwestern cuisine—just head to the Combine, where Albert Chow's serving up California-style fish tacos, sticky smoked ribs, and crispy buttermilk fried chicken. The Combine is the kind of place that brings a neighbourhood together. You can't lose when you order off the menu at the Combine, but this spot's gotten some serious attention for their ribs and is the three-time winner of Thrill of the Grill, a Danforth charity rib competition!

Dr. Laffa
Est. 2011 (relocated 2014)
3027 Bathurst St.
North York, ON M6B 3B5
(647) 352-9000
www.drlaffa.com

At Dr. Laffa you'll feel like you hit the jackpot. Food? Massive and tasty laffa sandwiches. Learning? Who knew that laffa bread is made by sticking dough to the inside of something called a "taboon"? Faves include the Falafel Laffa and shwarma. Who says a visit to the doctor can't be fun? At Dr. Laffa, the prescription is for a daily dose of delicious.

El Rincon
Est. 2003
653 St. Clair Ave. W
Toronto, ON M6C 1A7
(416) 656-1059
www.elrinconmexicano.ca

Get a little salsa in your step at El Rincon, *the* spot in Toronto to grab traditional Mexican food. And it's no wonder people like it. Jorge Morgado's serving some of the best tacos, burritos, empanadas, and sizzling fajitas in town—and don't forget the famous guacamole. Come on Thursday and you'll also walk into a Latin fiesta with a full-blown mariachi band. It's a little bit of Mexico making a big impact in Toronto!

Emma's Country Kitchen
Est. 2012
810 St. Clair Ave. W
Toronto, ON M6E 1A7
(416) 652-3662
www.emmascountrykitchen.com

Chef Rachel Pellett pays homage to her grandmother at Emma's Country Kitchen, a gingham-clad brunch spot nestled just north of Toronto's downtown core. Rachel makes everything from scratch and adds a whole lotta love to every dish. She regularly goes through over 2000 eggs, 75 pounds of butter, and 500 biscuits a week! Whether you're digging into Emma's Benny, served over her grandmother's original buttermilk biscuits, or spoiling your appetite with her award-winning fritters and doughnuts, you'll feel like you're right back on grandmother's farm.

Fancy Franks
Est. 2012
326 College St.
Toronto, ON M5T 1S3
(416) 920-3647
www.fancyfranks.com

Torontonians got their hot dogs from street vendors—until now! Everyone's high tailin' it to Fancy Franks for chef and owner Angelos Economopoulos's deliciously inventive dogs. Try one stuffed with Korean beef ribs and kimchi or a deep-fried Buffalo chicken wing dog. The name may be "fancy" but the franks are simply good. For dessert, have some mini doughnuts made fresh by their doughnut robot right before your eyes! Thanks, Doughnut Robot!

The Gabardine
Est. 2010
372 Bay St.
Toronto, ON M5H 2W9
(647) 352-3211
www.thegabardine.com

Homey lunch options in Toronto's financial district are few and far between, but nestled quietly among the skyscrapers lies a local gem: the Gabardine. Try chef Graham Pratt's chicken pot pie, a moment of casual comfort in the middle of your hectic day, or the Grilled Brined Pork Chop on Black-Eyed Pea Ragout with Sautéed Mustard Greens and Red Eye Gravy. Even the name of this dish is a mouthful. The Gabardine was Bay Street's best-kept secret—until now!

**Flank Steak Sandwich
(The Clubhouse Sandwich Shop)**

Chef Aki Urata (Kinton Ramen)

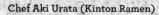

The Combine Eatery

Kare Kare Beef Stew (Casa Manila)

So-Cal Basa Taco (The Combine Eatery)

Yorkie Burger (The Borough)

Hogtown Smoke

Est. 2011
1959 Queen St. E
Toronto, ON M4L 1H7
(416) 691-9009
www.hogtownsmoke.ca

Hogtown Smoke is a popular Beaches destination for barbecue-bending smoked meats. Pitmaster Scott Fraser learned the ways of the smoker from barbecue virtuoso Aaron Franklin and, like his mentor, Scott isn't afraid to challenge convention. Scott is injecting chicken with tequila, cooking baked beans in root beer, and infusing pulled pork with Jack Daniels for the Jack'd Up Grilled Cheese. Get there quick or you'll miss the last rib at the Hogtown Smoke!

The Hogtown Vegan

Est. 2011
1056 Bloor St. W
Toronto, ON M6H 1M3
(416) 901-9779
www.hogtownvegan.com

When you think of vegan food, you can't help but think "healthy," right? Happily, the Hogtown Vegan embraces its deep-fried side as much as any good diner would, reinventing Southern soul food. What this joint lacks in flesh it makes up for in flavour, thanks to co-owners Madeleine Foote and Scott McCannell. It appeals to everyone: neighbourhood elders, punky teens, even carnivores. Faves include the Pulled "Pork" Sandwich and the Philly "Cheesesteak." Embrace your unmeat side! You'll be glad you did.

Kinton Ramen

Est. 2012
668 Bloor St. W
Toronto, ON M6G 1L2
(416) 551-8177
www.kintonramen.com

Some households were raised on boxed mac 'n' cheese, and others had chicken noodle soup. Many North Americans grew up eating loads of instant ramen noodle soup. At Kinton Ramen, chef Aki Urata's comfort food comes in the form of a big bowl of steamy, slurp-worthy noodles and rich and flavourful meats that are swimming in hearty slow-cooked broth. You'll never go back to packaged noodles! Take comfort in this energetic and friendly Japanese noodle house in the heart of Toronto.

La Cubana

Est. 2013
392 Roncesvalles Ave.
Toronto, ON M6R 2M9
(416) 538-7500
www.lacubana.ca

. . . .

Nestled in Toronto's bustling Roncesvalles neighbourhood is a bright and cheery spot specializing in flavourful contemporary takes on traditional Cuban diner food. La Cubana pays homage to owner Corinna Mazo's grandfather, who had his very own diner in Cuba. In his honour, she stuck to the retro theme, choosing bright aqua tiles and hanging orb light fixtures. Take a front-row seat at the counter and watch the chef happily dish up quick bocaditos, hand-held medianoches, and rice and bean dinners—and don't forget the cinnamon doughnuts!

Lahore Tikka House

Est. 1996
1365 Gerrard St. E
Toronto, ON M4L 1Z3
(416) 406-1668
www.lahoretikkahouse.com

. . . .

The riotous explosion of colours, sound, and fragrant smells may have you thinking you're at a South Asian wedding, but it's just another dinner service at Toronto's legendary Lahore Tikka House. Serving spectacularly authentic subconti-

nent dishes in a dining area resembling a sultan's tent, chef Gulshan Allibhai delivers not just a fantastic meal, but an experience! Locals in the heart of Toronto's Little India neighbourhood certainly know great curry when they taste it, and Lahore Tikka House is the real deal.

Lisa Marie

Est. 2013
638 Queen St. W
Toronto, ON M6J 1E4 Ð
(647) 748-6822
www.fidelgastros.com

. . . .

Toronto's pop-up king, Matt Basile, settles down at his permanent home with Lisa Marie to serve fun and over-the-top brunches that blur the line between street food and breakfast food. Try Matt's massive double breakfast burger with pancakes for buns, or his aptly named Naptime—a 6-ounce steak served on a baguette with bacon and two eggs! With a side of Matt's famous pad Thai fries, this is one breakfast you'll want to pull up a chair for.

Little Fin

Est. 2014
4 Temperance St.
Toronto, ON M5H 1Y5
(647) 348-7000
www.littlefin.ca

For a little East Coast comfort, head to Little Fin, a downtown Toronto spot serving some of the best seafood around! With tacos, salads, and sandwiches all loaded with shrimp, lobster, and fish, this joint will lure you in. Chef Michael Steh's making it all from scratch with ocean-fresh ingredients, shipping lobster in from Nova Scotia. Designed to look and feel like an East Coast cottage, Little Fin delivers a workday lunch worth remembering!

Loaded Pierogi

Est. 2014
1044 Gerrard St. E
Toronto, ON M4M 1Z8
(647) 348-0088
www.loadedpierogi.ca

At Loaded Pierogi, chef Adam Dolley uses homemade pierogies as the base for poutine-style creations. Your baba's never made pierogies quite like this before. With toppings like pulled pork, duck confit, and Buffalo chicken to choose from, you'll fall in love with pierogies all over again. Customers

attest that there are no bad choices. *Toronto Life* even credits their Cabbage Patch Kid dish as the best way to "get kids to stomach—and love— Brussels sprouts"! Hooray!

Mezes

Est. 1996
456 Danforth Ave.
Toronto, ON M4K 1P3
(416) 778-5150
www.mezes.com

At Greektown's Mezes, Tony and Marissa Pethakas welcome you into their family. Here you get the best that Mykonos has to offer with each mouthful of Mezes' flaming saganaki, fresh calamari, and homemade baklava, just like Yiayia used to make. It's traditional Greek, made to share, though we wouldn't blame you for hoarding Tony's kleftiko, which means "stolen." Steal a bite of this flaky phyllo pie, packed with garlicky roasted lamb leg, feta-studded spinach, and tomatoes. This dish is a felony-worthy feast.

Pizzeria Defina
Est. 2011
321 Roncesvalles Ave.
Toronto, ON M6R 2M6
(416) 534-4414
www.pizzeriadefina.com

. . . .

Take a trip around the world when you eat at Pizzeria Defina. Owner Roksolana Curkowskyj lets her staff get playful with pies inspired by seasonal produce and global cuisines. They're known for the unique Polish-inspired Pierogi Pizza. Sit and watch the pizzaiolos spin the dough high in the air and then bite into your own slice. Yum!

Pizzeria Via Mercanti
Est. 2006
188 Augusta Ave.
Toronto, ON M5T 1M1
(647) 343-6647
www.pizzeriaviamercanti.ca

. . . .

Toronto's Kensington Market is a long way from the old country, but it's *the* place to find pizza and pasta so good you'll feel like you're right smack dab in the middle of a piazza in Salerno! Naples transplant and pizzaiolo Romolo Salvati's just the guy to show you how it's done. He's rolling out homemade pasta topped with house-cured meats, and sliding crisp and chewy Neapolitan-style pizzas out of the oven and into your mouth! *Salute!*

Sanremo Bakery
Est. 1969
374 Royal York Rd.
Toronto ON M8Y 2R3
(416) 255-2808
www.sanremobakery.com

. . . .

Holding court on Royal York Road since 1969, this Italian bakery—especially renowned for its pastry—has been a stalwart of the neighbourhood and is still run by the Bozzo family. You can't miss with a quintessential Italian classic: Sicilian cannoli. It's a crispy shell of fried flaky dough filled with citrusy cream and topped with powdered sugar and maraschino cherries. But save room for some millefoglie cake. Meaning "thousand layer" cake, the name may be a slight over-exaggeration, but when you bite into the crisp buttery puff pastry layered with custard cream and fresh strawberries and decorated with chocolate-dipped profiteroles, you'll wish there were a couple hundred more layers to nibble on.

Doughnuts (La Cubana)

Lahore Tikka House

Sanremo Bakery

Lobster Roll (Little Fin)

Pizzeria Defina

Menes

Saturday Dinette
Est. 2014
807 Gerrard St. E
Toronto, ON M4M 1Y5
(416) 465-5959
www.saturdaydinette.com

Tucked away in Leslieville is Saturday Dinette, a welcoming neighbourhood diner where Suzanne Barr's cooking up cozy Caribbean-style diner food with a whole lotta heart. Suzanne plays vinyl on an old record player in the dining room, and can be seen working in the kitchen, often with her son Myles looking on. Grab a seat at the counter and Suzanne will serve you herself. Mounds of hot fried chicken, gooey coconut mac 'n' cheese, and massive beef-and-lamb burgers are sure to cure what ails you!

The Senator
Est. 1948
249 Victoria St.
Toronto, ON M5B 1V8
(416) 364-7517
www.thesenator.com

Toronto's oldest restaurant, the Senator has been serving hungry theatregoers classic diner dishes for the better part of a century—and not much has changed! The restaurant has the original fixtures and soda machines, giving the place a nostalgic feel. So grab a cozy booth and order the historic Senator burger with fries or opt for sumptuous homestyle dishes like braised short ribs. Every day is throwback day at the Senator.

Sky Blue Sky Sandwich Company
Est. 2009
605 Bloor St. W
Toronto, ON M6G 1K6
(647) 351-7945
www.sbssandwiches.com

Chad Comfort of Sky Blue Sky Sandwiches is obsessed with details, pairing bread and ingredients together like a master craftsman. A huge fan of the alternative pop band Wilco, Chad named his sandwich shop "Sky Blue Sky" after their 2007 album. Chad bakes his breads in-house for sandwiches like the pulled pork, served on cakey French bread, or the roast beef sandwich, served on Indian-inspired spicy Jack bread. Local in Toronto's Koreatown, Sky Blue Sky is all things sandwich!

Tich
Est. 2014
2314 Lake Shore Blvd. W
Etobicoke, ON M8V 1B5
(647) 349-8424
www.tich.ca
· · · · · · · · · ·

Get your Indian fix at Tich, a cheerful Mimico spot with two top-level chefs. Mandy Jawle cooks up naan and charred meats in their tandoor oven, and Sujoy Saha creates complex curries like butter chicken. Owner Karan Kalia

named the restaurant after Punjabi slang for "cool" and "stylish." To that effect, she decorated the place in modern dark wood, leather, a lit-up Tich sign, and hanging glass light fixtures. With its fantastic dishes and atmosphere, it's no wonder Tich is recognized throughout the entire city!

Uncle Betty's Diner
Est. 2011
2590 Yonge St.
Toronto, ON M4P 2J3
(416) 483-2590
www.unclebettys.com
· · · · · · · · · · · · ·

If fine dining is your gig, stay away from Uncle Betty's! At this boisterous family eatery, the food is as fun as the vibe. Owned by Samara Melanson and her husband, Robert Lewocz, Uncle Betty's is a Canadian original named after Samara's mom, an excellent cook with a tough side, who became a bit of a father figure to her nieces and nephews. Her nickname stuck. Enjoy the Ultimate Grilled Cheese or the famous Twink "eh," at a place where food and fun go together.

Pizzeria Via Mercanti

Pulled Pork Chimichanga (The Wren)

Corn Dog Doughnut (Von Doughnuts)

Macaroni and Cheese (Saturday Dinette)

Von Doughnuts

Est. 2013

713 Danforth Ave.

Toronto, ON M4J 1L2

(416) 901-8663

Witness dreams becoming reality at Von Doughnuts, where Jennifer Vaughan brings her sweet-tooth fantasies to life. Jennifer's creations come fried, filled, and topped with all manner of delights like chocolate bars, funnel cakes, pancakes, and even deep-fried pickles! If you can dream it, you can doughnut at Von Doughnuts. This Danforth hot spot goes through 440 pounds of flour and 450 eggs a week thanks to the families, kids, and doughnut freaks who come in search of kooky flavours.

The White Brick Kitchen

Est. 2012

641 Bloor St. W

Toronto, ON M6G 1K9

(647) 347-9188

www.thewhitebrickkitchen.com

Young chef Stephen Howell is already giving Mom a run for her money. With a menu focused on homespun flavours and subtle upgrades of Canadian classics, the White Brick Kitchen receives rave reviews from neighbourhood regulars and university kids missing Mom's kitchen. Try the savoury Turkey 'n' Biscuits or the fried chicken that's more Canadian than it is Deep South. White Brick Kitchen is a neighbourhood gem on a quiet stretch of Bloor.

The Wren

Est. 2013

1382 Danforth Ave.

Toronto, ON M4J 1M9

(647) 748-1382

www.thewrendanforth.com

At this pub-style neighbourhood joint on the Danforth, chef Jacob Taylor serves up spicy and sultry dishes inspired by Southern barbecue and Tex-Mex fare. Want a heap of pulled pork in your chimichanga? What about a good helping of barbecue char on your fried chicken? Like the migratory bird it's named for, the Wren brings some of the sunny South to the Great White North, where it's become a neighbourhood favourite worthy of Toronto's attention.

LOCAL GEMS

Bata Shoe Museum

Toronto is well known for its fascinating variety of museums, but if you're looking for something a little different, why not check out the Bata Shoe Museum? With over a thousand shoes on display from all over the world, this museum is sure to give shoe lovers something to swoon over. Their collection contains shoes from as far back as 4500 years ago, as well as an extensive array of footwear once worn by celebrities and historical figures. 327 Bloor St. W., Toronto, ON, M5S 1W7. www.batashoemuseum.ca.

The Bathrooms at Otto's Berlin Döner

Toronto is home to many strange attractions, but probably none more so than the unique bathrooms at Otto's Berlin Döner. Nestled inside this German street food restaurant located in Kensington Market are two single-use gender-neutral bathrooms with mysterious unmarked buttons attached to the wall. Press the blue button and your bathroom is turned into a disco; press the red button and you'll get a techno party. Each experience lasts 15 seconds and includes strobe lights, disco balls, and themed music. 256 Augusta Ave., Toronto, ON, M5T 2L9. www.ottosdoner.com.

The Biblio-Mat

Inside one of Toronto's most antiquarian bookshops, the Monkey's Paw, sits the Biblio-Mat, the world's first vending machine to randomly dispense used books. Boasting a wide selection of books to collect, for only $2 you can purchase your random 20th-century literary gem from this truly one-of-a-kind machine. While there, browse the store's special collections and take a look at their distinctive displays, including medical drawings on the walls and a stuffed crow perched atop a typewriter. 1267 Bloor St. W., Toronto, ON, M6H 1N7. www.monkeyspaw.com.

The Elgin and Winter Garden Theatre Centre

Located in the heart of downtown Toronto, this national historic site is the last of its kind. The double-decker theatre is known for putting on unique plays and musicals, but there's also an exclusive opportunity to view the history of the theatre. Tours are offered Thursdays and Saturdays for those interested in looking at the world's largest vaudeville scenery collection, a Simplex Silent Film Projector, and the theatre's unique backstage history, including artifacts from a bygone era. 189 Yonge St., Toronto, ON, M5B 1M4. www.heritagetrust.on.ca.

Ireland Park

Five bronze and limestone sculptures adorn Toronto's Lake Ontario harbourfront to commemorate the Irish famine migrants of 1847. The emotionally moving "Arrival" statues and the bleak landscape on which they rest symbolize the Ireland the hopeful immigrants left behind. Looking out towards the route the migrant ships took all those years ago, visitors can take in the site's great historical significance. Ireland Park, Queens Quay W., Toronto, ON, M5V 3G3. www.irelandparkfoundation.com.

Leslieville's Nutty Doll House

What started out as a small collection to help homeowner Shirley Sumaiser cope with the passing of her husband has quickly become one of Leslieville's unusual attractions. The small plot of land is covered from top to bottom in toy dolls, animals, and more. This ever-changing front lawn display is updated as holidays come and go, allowing for a different spectacle nearly every time you visit. Colloquially known as "the Doll House," this interesting home is the perfect spot for a fun family photoshoot. Take a stroll along Bertmount Avenue—you can't miss it.

Toronto Music Garden

Inspired by the works of legendary composer Johann Sebastian Bach and designed by world-renowned cellist Yo Yo Ma and landscape designer Julie Moir Messervy, the Toronto Music Garden is a harmonious collaboration between nature and music in one of Toronto's most beautiful urban parks. Open year-round, but especially active in the summer season, the garden acts as a musical hub and even offers concert series in various styles of music. 479 Queens Quay W., Toronto, ON, M5V 3M8. www.harbourfrontcentre.com/venues/torontomusicgarden.

The Toronto Necropolis

If you're looking to satisfy your morbid curiosity as well as get a taste of Gothic Revival architecture, look no further than the Toronto Necropolis. One of Toronto's oldest and most historic cemeteries, dating back to 1850, it features stained-glass windows, sculptures, and classic Victorian design. Browse through the cemetery grounds and see if you can spot the final resting places of some of Toronto's most prominent historical figures, like William Lyon Mackenzie, Jack Layton, Anderson Ruffin Abbott (the first Canadian-born black surgeon), and many more. 200 Winchester St., Toronto, ON, M4X 1B7.

Ward's Island

Thousands of visitors and locals alike flock to the Toronto Islands every year, but if you're looking to escape the crowds of Centre Island or Hanlan's Point, check out Ward's Island instead. It's the residential part of the island system so it's not quite as busy by comparison. Enjoy its picturesque beach, boardwalk, disc golf course, soccer field, and café—there's lots to do! Ward's Island, Toronto, ON. www.torontoisland.com/wards.php.

Home Sweet Home
John's Fave Local Eats

Guess what? I love eating out (shocking, I know). I loved eating out before I started hosting *You Gotta Eat Here!* and I still love eating out (and no, it *doesn't* feel like work). But I also love hanging out in my Toronto neighbourhood, because I love my neighbourhood. That and I'm lazy and don't feel like going to any other neighbourhood.

So when it comes to the eateries I frequent, most of them are close to home. Sure, my wife can occasionally talk me into venturing further afield. But creature of habit that I am, these are the places I visit with slightly alarming regularity. Here are my local haunts.

Tre Mari Bakery

Trips to Tre Mari may have become routine for me (you know you're a regular when they yell "See you tomorrow!" as you head out the door), but there's nothing routine about a place that's been in business for more than fifty years. Hell, I've been going there for at least forty.

Most of my trips to Tre Mari are for their ridiculously fresh panini (thank you, God, for turning my girls off sliced bread), but I can't resist their cannoli or Italian cold cuts. And they have a hot table where I might purchase the occasional veal parmigiana sandwich. Or arancini. Or any of their other delicious Italian specials.

Frank's Pizza House

My buddy George owns Frank's, another institution with a fifty-year history. And while its lineage may be confusing, the food is straight-up delicious. Yeah, I lie awake at night craving their pizzas and calzones . . . but it's the atmosphere I love, too.

So if it's a lazy day, I'll wander over to Frank's and simply sit at the bar and shoot the breeze with George while he makes pizzas. And I swear one day I'm jumping on the line and working with him.

More!

I realize I may be stereotyping myself with an Italian bakery and a pizza joint, but there's more to me than just tomato sauce and ricotta, okay? There's also **California Sushi**, a terrific little sushi restaurant that I've been known to visit once (or more!) a week. A *You Gotta Eat Here!* feature, **Emma's Country Kitchen** is dangerously close to my gym, so any calories I happen to burn go right back on with their all-day brunch. I love **El Rincon** (also featured on the show), a refreshingly authentic Mexican restaurant. And there's nothing like **Kinton Ramen**—which I discovered through the show—to warm your innards on a cold Toronto afternoon.

I know it seems like I eat out a lot. I do. But that's not all there is to John Catucci.

Sometimes I order in.

Kinton Ramen has five locations in Toronto, so I can pop in almost every time I'm out! Of course, there are all those other joints I love, too. . . .

WINDSOR, ON

Bubi's Awesome Eats
Est. 1977
620 University Ave. W
Windsor, ON N9A 5R5
(519) 252-2001
www.bubis.org

Vampires, consider yourselves warned. Owner Michael "Buddy" Miloyevich's infamous Bubi Sauce is so garlicky you'll smell like you bathed in it for days to come. You can't stop eating the stuff, and why would you want to? It goes on just about every delicious dish, from the Best of the Breast to a mind-numbing selection of burgers, like the Gonzo Burger and Bastien's Chili Cheez Train. There's something for everyone at Bubi's—just check your fangs at the door.

Mamo Burger Bar
Est. 2013
13430 Tecumseh Rd. E
Windsor, ON N8N 2L9
(519) 735-3999
www.mamoburgerbar.com

Ryan Odette, the mastermind behind Windsor's favourite barbecue joint (and *You Gotta Eat Here!* alum) Smoke & Spice, is back with a new restaurant concept: signature burgers! His menu packs in a lotta flavourful punches. Dig into gourmet burgers like the Daddy Mac with house-made mac 'n' cheese and smoked pulled pork atop fresh ground chuck. At Mamo, they don't take reservations—not even Ryan's own mother enjoys the privilege! Come early and come hungry because their double-patty burgers are a feast!

Motor Burger

Est. 2009
888 Erie St. E
Windsor, ON N9A 3Y9
(519) 252-8004
www.motorburger.ca

When the recession hit, Jay Souilliere and Gino Gesuale recognized that the market for fine dining was coming to an abrupt halt, and their high-end Italian restaurant NOI would have a hard time surviving. Rather than close down, Jay and Gino simply switched gears. Motor Burger—a gourmet joint paying homage to Windsor's rich automotive history—was born. Casual and warm, it's unpretentious and inventive. Try the Fire Bird, Autostrada, Lamb-orghini, or Deux Chevaux.

Rino's Kitchen

Est. 2010
131 Elliott St. W
Windsor, ON N9A 4N4
(519) 962-8843
www.rinoskitchen.com

At Rino's Kitchen it's all about cozy classic dishes, like waffles covered in house-cured pork and linguini carbonara. Locals find comfort in every aspect of eating in this quaint historic Essex County house. Chef Rino Bortolin's devotion to good food transcends his being a chef.

In order to share his passion, the restaurant offers cooking classes for adults and also for children. If he wasn't already busy enough, Rino now serves as a city councillor for the City of Windsor. Talk about civic-minded!

Smoke & Spice Southern Barbeque

Est. 2008
7470 Tecumseh Rd. E
Windsor, ON N8T 1E9
(519) 252-4999
www.smokenspice.com

Owners Ryan and Tina Odette love barbecue so much that they trained with pit boss Pat Martin in Nolensville, Tennessee, before opening their own place. From the outside, Smoke & Spice looks like an Alberta ranch house. The inside is laid-back and homey, and everyone feels like family. Feast on Ryan's St. Louis cut spare ribs. If you're wondering what that smoky smell is, follow your nose to the end of the rainbow and find the treasure at Smoke & Spice.

The Twisted Apron
Est. 2011
1833 Wyandotte St. E
Windsor, ON N8Y 1E2
(519) 256-2665
www.thetwistedapron.com

Windsor is well known for its breakfast buffets, but the Twisted Apron is the place where locals go to eat really, really good food and to try things they've never eaten before. With dishes like the Breakfast Poutine, featuring scrambled eggs and Southern-style sausage gravy, or Truffled Grilled Cheese, "all you can eat" simply can't compete! The Twisted Apron is filled with the comforts of home. It's all about connecting with friends and family over great food.

LOCAL GEMS

B.V.'s House of Pong

If you're looking for a nice, family-friendly indoor activity, check out B.V.'s House of Pong, Windsor's only table tennis social club. Ten ping pong tables are available to rent by the hour or half hour for less than $20 a table. They also have theme nights from Monday to Thursday: Monday's $5 "all you can play" between 7 and 11 p.m., "two for Tuesday" (their version of two-for-one night), Wednesday's beer night (one hour of play and four beers for $28), and Thursday's "bring your own vinyl" (show off your personal record collection!). 511 Ouellette Ave., Windsor, ON, N9A 4J3. www.bvshouseofpong.com.

Walkerville Brewery Tour

For only $7 per person you can go an interesting tour of Windsor's Walkerville Brewery, learning the history and production practices of a brewery that has been a staple in the city since 1890. Taste samples of various brews and enjoy a 12-ounce glass of your choice. Make sure to call ahead to reserve your time slot because they can fill up quickly. 525 Argyle Rd., Windsor, ON, N8Y 4Z8. www.walkervillebrewery.com.

Windsor-Style Pizza

When it comes to pizza styles, don't settle for New York or Chicago. Did you know that there's a famous style a little closer to home? Hailed as the third-best pizza in the world, Armando's has made Windsor the pizza capital Canada never knew it had. If you're looking to get a good taste of what Windsor has to offer, make sure you grab a slice from this world-renowned family pizza place. Armando's (Dine-In), 326 Cabana Rd. E., Windsor, ON, N9G 1A3; Armando's Pizza, 9150 Riverside Dr. E., Windsor, ON, N8S 1H1; Armando's Pizza, 3202 Walker Rd., Windsor, ON, N8W 3R8. www.armandospizza.com.

EASTERN
CANADA

CAPE BRETON ISLAND, NS, AND SURROUNDING AREA

Charlene's Bayside Restaurant and Cafe
Est. 2008
9657 Highway 105
Whycocomagh, NS B0E 3M0
(902) 756-8004

· · · · · · · · · · ·

Whycocomagh is one of the first places we ever visited on haunt- ingly beautiful Cape Breton Island. It's also home to Charlene's and their Bucket of Mud, what all desserts want to be when they grow up. But there's more here than just the sweet stuff. Charlene's son (and chef) Elliot makes a mean lobster roll, seafood chowder, and fish cake, all favoured by locals. By the time you've finished your meal, chances are you'll have made a few new friends, too—maybe even Charlene herself!

Colette's Place
Est. 1982
201 Brookside St.
Glace Bay, NS B1A 1L6
(902) 849-8430

· · · · · · · · · · ·

Warm hearts are a specialty at Colette's Place, a family affair that puts people first. Little has changed but the name since 1982, when Judy McKinnon, Colette's mother, opened it. Now Colette and her husband, Frankie Martin, run the restaurant, ensuring love is in every bite of the signature BBQ Sausage Dinner. Karen Bran, grandmother to seven, enjoys making desserts so much she does it for nothing, but her creations taste like a million bucks. Don't be embarrassed by the butterscotch pie on your face. You're among family!

Flavor 19
Est. 2011
Lingan Golf Course
1225 Grand Lake Rd.
Sydney, NS B1M 1A2
(905) 562-2233
www.cbflavor.com/flavornineteen

. . . .

John's no golfer. But show him a terrific golf-course restaurant and he'll buy a pair of knickers and start wearing polo shirts instead of plaid. Flavor 19 has been making a splash in Sydney's dining scene since 2011. Owner and chef Scott Morrison knows what people like to eat and dreams big. There are—you guessed it—nineteen flavours of wings, but John's fave is Root Beer. A culinary hole-in-one!

LOCAL GEMS

Broughton Ghost Town

An interesting piece of Nova Scotia history, Broughton was meant to be one of Canada's first planned towns. It was under development during the early 1900s, but when the mining company went bankrupt, the town was never finished. The incomplete town was host to the Broughton Arms Hotel, which had the very first revolving door in North America. Currently, little remains other than crumbling foundations and structures, but it holds the title of Cape Breton's very own ghost town. Broughton Rd., Cape Breton Island, NS.

FireHouse Ironworks

Tucked away in the small town of Whycocomagh on Cape Breton Island lies FireHouse Ironworks, a traditional blacksmith shop that specializes in ironwork, stainless steel, aluminum, and mixed-media products. Not only do they have a shop with unique hand-crafted products available for purchase, but you can even take a crash course on basic blacksmithing. One-day packages range from one to four hours and allow you to create and take home your own handmade item. FireHouse Ironworks, 109 Main St., Whycocomagh, Cape Breton Island, NS, B0E 3M0. www.firehouseironworks.com.

CHARLOTTETOWN, PEI

The Churchill Arms
Est. 2003
75 Queen St.
Charlottetown, PEI C1A 4A8
(902) 367-3450
www.churchillarms.ca

. . . .

At Charlottetown's answer to merry old England, you'll find the delicious curries Brits adore and pints to share with friends and family. It's all thanks to British expat Francine Thorpe, who immigrated to PEI and brought her grandmother's recipes with her. Her mellow butter chicken and onion bhaji are a curry rookie's dream. Don't get up in arms; head *to* the Arms. The Churchill Arms, that is.

Famous Peppers
Est. 2003 (relocated 2011)
202 Kent St.
Charlottetown, PEI C1A 1P2
(902) 370-7070
www.famouspeppers.ca

. . . .

Serving "the very best pizza on the island" according to PEI's superstar chef Michael Smith, Charlottetown's Famous Peppers is famous for their unique pies. Vivacious chef Jocelyne Mitchell subs out standard tomato sauce for maple cream on the Spud Islander, and transforms the East Coast donair into an Island cult classic. When it comes to one-of-a-kind, kooky creations, Jocelyne shines in this family-owned spot that radiates with that special Island pride.

Water-Prince Corner Shop and Lobster Pound
Est. 1991
141 Water St.
Charlottetown, PEI C1A 1A8
(902) 368-3212
www.waterprincelobster.ca

. . . .

Owned by PEI native Shane Campbell, the Water-Prince Corner Shop and Lobster Pound has made its imprint by following this philosophy: "Keep it simple, keep it fresh, and you'll keep them happy." Lines form early for homemade seafood chowder, fresh biscuits, and the two-pound monsters they serve . . . and ship everywhere. It's the real deal. Sure, you can order a burger instead and prompt a local to say, "You're a CFA, aren't you?" (That's "come from away," don't ya know.)

LOCAL GEMS
Attend a Ceilidh

PEI is known for is its rich history of folk music, and there's nowhere better to experience it than at a classic PEI ceilidh or "kitchen party." Gather round at local homes, halls, or churches to listen to some foot-stomping classic folk music. Featuring fiddles, pianos, step dancing, singing, and lots of good food, ceilidhs are a great introduction to the PEI community and its lively culture. www.ceilidhs.ca.

Lighthouse Tours

You can get just about anywhere in PEI within a day, so why not take the day to tour the coastal lighthouses? Eight lighthouses located across Prince Edward Island are open to the public and easily accessible from the highways. The lighthouses at West Point, Victoria Rangelight, Wood Islands, Cape Bear, Point Prim, Panmure Head, East Point, and Souris all have stories to tell and museums on-site where you can learn their rich histories. www.tourismpei.com/pei-lighthouses.

Island Time
All the Time

News flash: Canada is full of wonderful people. As a matter of fact, I think it's probably mandatory that to become a Canadian citizen you have to pass some sort of kindness test. ("You see an elderly woman struggling with her groceries. As you approach her, you decide to: a) help her with her bags, b) walk her to her car, c) adopt her, or d) all of the above.") But if you want to find the highest percentage of kind, generous, and friendly folks anywhere, head to the Maritimes.

Maritimers show their love in lots of ways, but for a guy from Toronto—where life usually operates at warp speed—I really feel it when walking down a Maritime street. No matter where I go when I'm there, from Halifax to St. John's, perfect strangers greet me on the street with a hearty "Good morning!" or "How are you?" Hell, they even make *eye contact*. (Okay, so that one threw me a bit, but I got used to it.)

The Maritimes is also the best place on earth to jaywalk, yet another testament to the kindness of its residents. Drivers there are so jaywalk-friendly that they'll actually *stop* in the middle of the road and wave you across in front of them! Even if you're walking on the side of the road and the *thought* of jaywalking crosses your mind, cars will stop in anticipation of it. "You look like you want to jaywalk, sir. And I'm going to stop my car for you . . . just in case."

In fact, things have gotten so bad (or good, depending on your point of view) that Charlottetown's police chief recently went on record asking drivers to stop being so damn polite to one another. Seems they were stopping in the middle of the road to let other drivers enter the flow of traffic only to be hit from behind!

Yep, it's a classic Canadian conundrum, folks. But I think the good people of PEI will be able to work it out. And nicely, too.

Have I mentioned that Maritimers sometimes show love by stuffing inordinate amounts of buttery lobster and other delicious seafood into your face? Exhibit A is right behind me.

2 Doors Down
Est. 2013
1533 Barrington St.
Halifax, NS B3J 3X7
(902) 422-4224
www.go2doorsdown.com

The top of the menu at 2 Doors Down says "local pocket-friendly fresh made with love," and chef Craig Flinn is a man of his word. This come-as-you-are neighbourhood restaurant serves up great homestyle dishes like smoked potato chowder and braised beef short rib at affordable prices. In keeping with its casual theme, you'll eat up all that delicious food on rustic farm doors. Come one, come hungry! You're sure to be delighted.

The Armview Restaurant & Lounge
Est. 1951
7156 Chebucto Rd.
Halifax, NS B3L 1N4
(905) 455-4395
www.thearmview.com

This Halifax gem has been serving up the freshest seafood money can buy for more than sixty years, so it's no surprise their motto is "Straight from the shore to our door!" By restoring the interior to echo the original diner's flair, childhood friends and current owners George Kapetanakis, Peter Tsuluhas, and Billy Nikolaou have created a retro-chic atmosphere to match the menu. Fish isn't all you'll find. Day or night, there's always something new and good to try!

Boneheads BBQ
Est. 2010
1014 Barrington St.
Halifax, NS B3H 2P9
(902) 407-4100
www.lickthebone.com

In a place where seafood is king, you'd never expect to find

Southern barbecue. Owner Cindy Wheatley's friends called her a *bonehead* for introducing an alien cuisine to fish-eating Haligonians, but she believed so strongly in the cuisine that she named her restaurant in honour of their skepticism. Now they apologize with every bite of Boneheads' pulled pork. The smoked chicken wings are another showstopper. Like it slow and low (and can't possibly eat another bite of lobster)? Boneheads is your place.

Hali Deli
Est. 2011
2389 Agricola St.
Halifax, NS B3K 4B8
(902) 406-2500
www.halideli.com

. . . .

With nary a Jewish deli in Halifax, Sybil Fineberg realized the only way to get her friends to stop *kvetching* about it was to open one of her own! She serves up family recipes like her Aunt Lil's sweet and sour cabbage balls and her mother's loaded latkes to crowds of happy diners. Try the dish Sybil laughingly calls her Old World Smoked Meat Potato Pot, a "heart attack in a bowl." It's a *chagiga* in your mouth!

Morris East
Est. 2007
5212 Morris St.
Halifax, NS B3J 1B4
(902) 444-7663
www.morriseast.com

. . . .

What happens when you combine a wood-fired oven and brunch? Big Breakfast Pizza, that's what! Chef Sandy Cooley created the entire brunch menu at Morris East with the wood-burning oven in mind. There's no greasy flat top here, and hey, who doesn't love eating breakfast next to a cozy fire? And don't forget everybody's campfire favourite: s'mores! Sandy makes his graham crackers and marshmallows from scratch. You'll definitely want s'more of this dessert!

Salvatore's Pizzaiolo Trattoria
Est. 1994
5541 Young St.
Halifax, NS B3K 1Z7
(902) 455-1133
www.salvatorespizza.ca

. . . .

A good pizza starts with the basics but mastering the nuances of crust-sauce-cheese is not easy. Fortunately, chef and owner Chris

Cuddihy has it down to a *T*. When Salvatore's New York Pizza closed, Chris kept its traditions alive by bringing the name and recipes back to Halifax, with great success: Salvatore's is consistently voted by local magazines as having the best pizza in town. Purists love the Original Pizza, but if you think a Halifax meal isn't complete without seafood, try the Clam Pie Marinato. We bet it'll get your vote, too!

LOCAL GEMS

Eat a Famous Halifax Donair

Originally introduced to Halifax by Greek immigrant Peter Gamoulakos, the donair is a delectable twist on classic Greek cuisine. Usually served in a pita, the donair features beef mixed with a blend of spices. It's cooked on a rotating spit, then shaved off and heated on a grill. A special sweet sauce kicks up the overall flavour. To try out this Maritime delicacy, visit King of Donair, the place where it all started in 1973. 6420 Quinpool Rd., Halifax, NS, B3L 1A8. www.kingofdonair.ca.

Freak Lunchbox

Inspired by the fascinating world of circuses and roadside attractions, Freak Lunchbox serves up a quirky blend of candy, carnival-style food, and fun. With a wide selection of odd and unusual candy as well as classics everyone knows and loves, this shop is the perfect place to satisfy your sweet tooth. Additionally, all of the shop's signs are hand painted and designed locally in Halifax. The store has even franchised across the Maritimes and into Quebec and Alberta, so you know it's got to be good! 1729 Barrington St., Halifax, NS, B3J 2A4. www.freaklunchbox.com.

Loaded Latkes (Hali Deli)

Wood-fired S'more (Morris East)

The Armview

Pulled Pork (Boneheads BBQ)

Wood-fired
oven in action
(Morris East)

Freak Lunchbox

LUNENBURG, NS

Magnolia's Grill
Est. 1987
128 Montague St.
Lunenburg, NS B0J 2C0
(902) 634-3287
www.magnolias-grill.com

. . . .

Combine some of the best eats on the East Coast with a stroll back through time by visiting Magnolia's in old-town Lunenburg, a UNESCO World Heritage Site since 1995. Magnolia's is Lunenburg at its best, and Lunenburg *is* seafood. Owner and chef Nancy Lohnes does seafood up right, beginning with her signature fish cakes. But the dish that stole John's heart was the popular lobster linguini, a meal so good you'll want to kiss the chef. As a matter of fact, John did!

Salt Shaker Deli
Est. 2006
124 Montague St.
Lunenburg, NS B0J 2C0
(902) 640-3434
www.saltshakerdeli.com

. . . .

This great little spot is shaking up life in Lunenburg with its fun, fresh, and local approach to seafood. Chefs Martin Salvador and Dawn Conrad are reeling in everyone from Lunenburg locals to tourists with their delicious smoked salmon club sandwiches and their hefty lobster rolls. The simple, bright dining room with beautiful views of the historic harbour make this place the quintessential Nova Scotia dining experience!

LOCAL GEM

Terra Beata Cranberry Farm

Stop by Terra Beata Cranberry Farm for a wide selection of cranberry products and a look at cranberry farm life. Everyone here is more than willing to answer your cranberry questions and tell you all about farming these tart crimson jewels. From September to November you can even try your hand at picking your own cranberries, an experience unique to Terra Beata (it's true: no other cranberry farm in Nova Scotia lets you pick your own!). 161 Monk Point Rd., Lunenburg, NS, B0J 2C0. cranberryfarm.ca

MONCTON, NB

Catch 22 Lobster Bar
Est. 2011
589 Main St.
Moncton, NB E1C 1C6
(506) 855-5335
www.catch22lobsterbar.com

Longtime friends Marc Surette and Denis Landry had always dreamt of opening a restaurant, but it took a while for everything to come together. Catch 22 Lobster Bar was worth the wait. They take classic comfort dishes and reinvent them lobster-style. Oddly, they named the restaurant before they decided to offer twenty-two lobster dishes, but there's nothing odd about the Lobster Florentine or the Blackened Cajun Lobster Jambalaya. They're simply delicious!

Tide & Boar Gastropub
Est. 2011
700 Main St.
Moncton, NB E1C 1E4
(506) 857-9118
www.tideandboar.com

Almost every Canadian pub serves poutine, but how many serve it with hunks of slow-roasted boar? That's the kind of surprise that awaits you at the Tide & Boar, where the food is as important as the spirits. Owners Matt Pennell and Chad Steeves know how to strike the perfect balance between booze and beast. John also loved their Polenta Fries and the Beeramisu. The eats here are never . . . *boaring*. That was really bad—sorry! (Not sorry enough to take it out, though.)

LOCAL GEM

Moncton Tidal Bore

Watch the waves roll backwards against the currents of the Petitcodiac River—a bizarre, must-see phenomenon. Years ago, these waves could often reach several metres in height, but the construction of a causeway in 1968 redirected water flow, diminishing their size. The causeway was removed in 2010, and the waves are slowly gaining height. Bore View Park, Bendview Ct., Moncton, NB, E1C 0H7. www.tourismnewbrunswick.ca/Products/T/TidalBore.aspx.

Tide & Boar Gastropub

Polenta Fries (Tide & Boar Gastropub)

Lobster Florentine (Catch 22 Lobster Bar)

Catch 22 Lobster Bar

Chafe's Landing
Est. 2008
11 Main Rd., Petty Harbour
St. John's, NL A0A 3H0
(709) 747-0802
www.chafeslanding.com

Chafe's Landing is as traditional as Newfoundland itself and a warm, comforting joint that serves up the best that the Rock has to offer. In a house built in 1878, Todd and Angela Chafe, like their ancestors, offer a mix of local seafood and game. Todd starts his work day at 3:00 a.m., when he catches the fish you'll eat for dinner. No wonder the fish and chips are so popular! This place is a *You Gotta Eat Here!* Fan Favourite.

LOCAL GEM

Herbie's Olde Craft Shoppe

Built in 1933, Herbie's was Petty Harbour's first grocery store, and the interior and ambience haven't changed since. What have changed are the products: Instead of shelves stocked with groceries, they're lined with quality Newfoundland crafts made by local artists. With just about any handcraft you can imagine—from quilts to pottery to jewellery and more—this historic building delivers a true taste of Newfoundland, old and new. 8 Long Run Rd., Goulds, NL, A1S 1N9.

SAINT JOHN, NB

Saint John Ale House
Est. 2003
1 Market Sq.
Saint John, NB E2L 4Z6
(506) 657-2337
www.saintjohnalehouse.com

. . . .

Saint John Ale House is one of John's all-time, hands-down, rock-solid favourite places. Fun, adventurous, and kind, Jesse Vergen and Peter Stoddart are its heart and soul, serving you delicious food like the buttermilk fried chicken. Wash it down with the largest beer selection in the area. People from far and wide come for a glass of their exclusive Moosehead Cask Ale—a one-of-a-kind experience, like the Ale House itself.

Taco Pica Restaurant
Est. 1993
96 Germain St.
Saint John, NB E2L 2E7
(506) 633-8492
www.tacopica.ca

. . . .

A taste of Guatemala in New Brunswick! Serving delicious dishes, from their vibrant salsa verde to spicy beef pepian, Flor and Fernando Bergel have been introducing Latin American flavours to the good people of Saint John for years. The bright colours and flavours of Guatemala are longtime favourites. Back in 1993, most Taco Pica customers were Latin immigrants, but over the years, the clientele has diversified. Twenty years and a town full of fans later, Taco Pica is more popular than ever.

Urban Deli
Est. 2009
68 King St.
Saint John, NB E2L 1G4
(506) 652-3354
www.urbandeli.ca

. . . .

Inspired by Montreal's Schwartz's Deli, Elizabeth Rowe toured some of North America's most famous delis, learning secrets from the masters. She now adds her own distinctive twists at the Urban. There's something here for the sandwich lover in all of us, from smoked meat to meatloaf, Reuben to triple-decker grilled cheese. Sit down at the 15-foot, 150-year-old communal table—a great place to meet new friends, catch up with old ones, and realize that we're all part of something bigger than ourselves.

Chef Jesse Vergen (Saint John Ale House)

Urban Deli

Ches's Famous Fish & Chips
Est. 1951
9 Freshwater Rd.
St. John's, NL A1C 2N1
(709) 726-2373
www.chessfishandchips.ca

. . . .

When it comes to fish and chips, Ches Barbour spoiled the people of St. John's. For years, he caught fresh fish every morning and cooked it up for eager customers every night. Although Ches and his wife, Betty, have since passed on, this family business continues to wow happy diners. They'll serve you something other than fish and chips, if you're *that* kind of person. But when everyone you ask about fish and chip in St. John's points to the iconic blue building on Freshwater Road, why would you want that?

Piatto Pizzeria
Est. 2010
377 Duckworth St.
St. John's, NL A1C 1H8
(709) 726-0909
www.piattopizzeria.com

. . . .

Authenticity and accessibility are key at Piatto Pizzeria, St. John's only certified Neapolitan pizza restaurant. Pizzaiolo Brian Vallis trained with pros in Vera Pizza Napoletana (VPN) schools, both in Naples, Italy, and California. He and his family then introduced Newfoundlanders to the pie he fell in love with, and they haven't been able to get enough of its trademark thin crust. Piatto is an important part of the community, even encouraging customers to submit their own pizza ideas. Try the Stephanie!

Rocket Bakery and Fresh Food
Est. 2011
272 Water St.
St. John's, NL A1C 1B7
(709) 738-2011
www.rocketfood.ca

. . . .

When Kelly and Mark Mansell opened the warm, inviting Rocket Bakery, the friendly light of St. John's started shining a little brighter. The 120-year-old building's cool vintage vibe adds to the experience, as do the sounds coming from inside on Tuesdays, when the Rocket hosts a kitchen party, a traditional Newfie jam session. Foodwise, there's enough variety to satisfy the pickiest tastes, from sweet to spicy, local to continental. Try the sausage rolls and the Lamb and Stout Pie. This is what love is supposed to feel like.

YellowBelly Brewery
Est. 2008
288 Water St.
St. John's, NL A1C 5J9
(709) 757-3784
www.yellowbellybrewery.com

. . . .

Situated in a historic building from the early 1600s—one of North America's oldest—YellowBelly Brewery is St. John's only gastro-brewpub. With a focus on cooking up classics like burgers and pizzas with a modern flare, owner Brenda O'Reilly often collaborates with her multicultural team of chefs to add globally influenced items like Sausage and Provolone Arancini and Marinated Chicken Lettuce Wraps to the menu.

LOCAL GEMS

Inside Outside Battery

With a simple download, you can get an insider's take on the Battery, one of Newfoundland's most iconic neighbourhoods. The Inside Outside Battery app tracks you via GPS, while prominent Newfoundland figures and locals narrate stories about the neighbourhoods you're walking through. So download the free app, enable GPS, plug in your headphones, and start exploring. www.twinestore .wixsite.com/insideoutsidebattery.

Puffin Watching

Get a look at one of Atlantic Canada's most unique animals: the Atlantic puffin, one of only four puffin species in the world. You can watch these unique little birds at the Witless Bay Ecological Reserve, which consists of four islands—Gull Island, Green Island, Great Island, and Pee Pee Island—and is home to North America's largest puffin colony (population: over 620,000). Several boat tours are available to take you on an adventure to watch the birds frolic on the cliffs and in the ocean, and you may even spot other wildlife along the way. Division No. 1, Subd. U, NL. www.env.gov.nl.ca/env/parks /wer/r_wbe.

Terry Fox Mile 0 Site

Canadians young and old know the name Terry Fox, the determined young man who lost his leg to cancer and set out on a cross-country run to raise awareness and funds for cancer research. See where it all began at Mile 0 in St. John's, Newfoundland, where on April 12, 1980, Terry dipped his artificial leg in the Atlantic Ocean and set off on his Marathon of Hope. The site features a sculpture that captures this iconic Canadian moment, among other items of historical relevance. 1 Water St., St. John's, NL, A1C 1A1. www.pc.gc.ca/APPS/CP-NR /release_e.asp?bgid=1623&andor1=bg.

Gettin' Back to Nature
Lobsters and Moose and Grizzlies ... Oh My!

Among the crew of *You Gotta Eat Here!*, I'm known as The Lobster Whisperer. Okay, so perhaps that's a bit of a stretch ... like a *huge* stretch.

The truth is, wildlife scares me. Oh, I'm okay with wildlife when it's served to me as part of a delicious meal. But *live* wildlife? That's a whole other kettle of fish.

Take lobster, for example. I don't know how many of you have dealt with live lobster, but let me assure you that they're big and ugly and dangerous (hey, they don't wear rubber bands for nothing!). Yet for some reason, the crew loves when I interact with them on air, so I've had to master the art of lobster taming. Now I know that rubbing a certain spot on the back of a lobster's head will calm the critter into a state of near-sleep. Hell, I can even make a lobster do a headstand! And they sure do taste good with drawn butter, too.

But my wildlife experience doesn't end with crustaceans, my friends. I'm big with *Mammalia*, too. In Churchill, Manitoba, the crew and I ventured out to the wreckage of an old cargo plane, where polar bears like to hang out when not hunting seals. And lo and behold, there they were! Sure, we kept a safe and respectful distance, but I made sure to abide by the law of the wild: You don't have to be the *fastest* guy in the group when you're spending time around creatures that can kill you, just make sure you're not the *slowest*.

That rule also came into play during an off day in British Columbia. Our hotel was connected to a driving range, and we decided to kill time by hitting some balls. As we walked towards the range, a hotel employee called out to us.

Him: "Hey, be careful out there. A grizzly's been hanging out by hole number seven."

Us: "Umm . . . Okay. Thanks?"

Although my first inclination was to stay inside, we eventually ventured outdoors. And although we never saw the bear, I did learn something: It's impossible to hit a golf ball well when your butt cheeks are tensed up as tight as a drum.

Wildlife can be scary even when you're in a vehicle . . . especially when that wildlife is a moose in Nova Scotia (where moose grow *really* big). That's probably why Nova Scotians go out of their way to warn visitors about the dangers of running into a moose, which is exactly what happened to us as we prepared to leave the town of Ingonish after shooting one evening.

As we negotiated a sharp bend in the road, we saw two headlights ahead that suddenly stopped moving. In an instant someone screamed "Oh, crap!" (They actually said the *S*-word. I'm just trying to keep it clean for the kids, okay?) "MOOSE!" The prophecy had come true.

Luckily, we didn't hit the moose, but it freaked out as we drove by, trapped between our van and the guardrail. The moose tried to leap over the van, but only managed to crash into the side a few times. Meanwhile, all of us inside the van were losing our freakin' minds, and Jim (who was driving) tried to keep us—and the moose—alive.

As for the moose, it walked away from the encounter unscathed. Me? Well, let's just say that I'm happy to enjoy big-city life for a while.

Yep, that's Alces alces (I know things). They don't taste as good as lobster.

**Rick's Fish 'n' Chips &
Seafood House**
Est. 1992
5544 Route 2
St. Peter's Bay, PEI C1A 2A0
(902) 961-3438
www.ricksfishnchips.com

. . . .

There's nothing pretentious about Rick or the restaurant that bears his name. Rick, his wife, Seana, and their team all hold true to one common cause: combining fresh, simple, and delicious seafood with good old-fashioned hospitality. One fave is the Cajun Mussels, steamed, dipped in Rick's "old English man" batter, then fried. Rick's is all about crispy pieces of fish enjoyed out on the deck on a warm summer afternoon. It's this down-hominess that makes Rick's a PEI legend.

LOCAL GEM

The Phoenix: Antiques and Oddities

PEI is full of quirky and interesting locations, which is why the Phoenix is a must-see. Packed wall-to-wall with over 400 items on display, this antique and oddity shop is sure to capture your attention. Whether you're looking for classic antiques like old books, china, or furniture, or want to venture over to the odd side and come away with something truly unique, you'll definitely find something to love. 5599 Route 2, St. Peter's Bay, PEI, C0A 2A0. www.thephoenixpei.com.

Gasthof Old Bavarian Restaurant
Est. 1985
1130 Knightville Rd.
Sussex, NB E4G 1E7
(506) 433-4735
www.oldbavarian.ca

· · · · · · · · · · · · · ·

Since 1985, the Gasthof Old Bavarian Restaurant has had New Brunswickers packing up the kids and heading to the countryside for hefty helpings of chef Claudia Giermindl's fresh, home-cooked Bavarian fare. With a farm, butcher shop, and restaurant all in one place, the trip from family farm to restaurant table doesn't get shorter than this! Open only on Fridays, Saturdays, and Sundays, Gasthof is a destination for a hearty weekend meal just like at *Oma*'s house.

LOCAL GEM
Mural Capital of Atlantic Canada

The local history of Sussex is captured on building walls across the region via more than twenty murals created by internationally renowned artists. Visitors can embark on self-guided tours through the town with the aid of a printed guide that details each mural and artist. Discover the history of Sussex from its start as a Maliseet community to its present-day standing as a beloved New Brunswick community. www.sussexmurals.com.

VICTORIA-BY-THE-SEA, PEI

Landmark Café
Est. 1989
12 Main St.
Victoria-by-the-Sea, PEI C0A 2G0
(902) 658-2286
www.landmarkcafe.ca

. . . .

The family-run Landmark Café offers everything its name promises and more. Owner Eugene Sauvé is its heart and soul, a veritable nutty professor in the kitchen who dreams up, tests, and re-tests his recipes for years. John loved his Meat Lover's Lasagna—just don't tell his Zia Felicetta, okay? No PEI restaurant located this close to the sea would offer a menu devoid of fish, and Landmark answers this call, too, with its delicious fresh haddock special. Don't miss the Landmark's unique culinary delights.

LOCAL GEMS

By-the-Sea Kayaking: Clam Up!

If you have time to take a kayak tour of picturesque Victoria-by-the-Sea, you can go on a clam dig using traditional methods, some of which date back centuries! When you get back to shore, your guides at By-the-Sea Kayaking will prepare a beachside feast like no other. You'll need it, having worked up an appetite with all that kayaking!
1 Water St., Victoria, PEI, C0A 2G0.
www.bytheseakayaking.ca.

NORTHERN CANADA

WHITEHORSE, YT

Antoinette's Food Cache
Est. 2006
4121 4th Ave.
Whitehorse, YT Y1A 1H7
(867) 668-3505
www.antoinettesfoodcache.ca

. . . .

Antoinette Oliphant's take on Caribbean comfort dishes has carved out a reputation that spans the Yukon territory. Here you get heaping homemade meals that warm the bellies of both devoted locals and international tourists. For cold Whitehorse winter days, there's nothing like Spicy Caribbean Pork or the Squash and Lentil Sweet Chili Stew with Rack of Lamb. Try the Tobagonian-Style Sweet Potato Pie for dessert. The Caribbean awaits in this northern town near the 60th parallel!

Klondike Rib & Salmon
Est. 1994
2116 2nd Ave.
Whitehorse, YT Y1A 1B9
(867) 667-7554
www.klondikerib.com

. . . .

Everything is big in the Yukon. Exhibit A: the portions and personalities at Dona Novecosky's Klondike Rib & Salmon. In the oldest operating building in Whitehorse, the Klondike is a tribute to the men and women who made the Gold Rush one of the most exciting times in Canadian history. The menu offers enough items to keep you working long into the night, including Wild Elk Stroganoff and the bison striploin. There's still gold in the Yukon, and it's served up daily here.

LOCAL GEM

Aroma Borealis Herb Shop

Using the northern boreal forest as inspiration, Aroma Borealis is a local herb shop that creates its own products by combining essential oils, herbs, and wild plants native to the Arctic. A range of all-natural herbal teas, bath salts, skin-care products, and more are available for purchase at reasonable prices. Store-owner Beverley Gray and her staff can also teach you how to use the power of herbs to better your mind, body, and spirit. 504-B Main St., Whitehorse, YK, Y1A 2B9. www.aromaborealis.com.

Glorious from Coast to Coast

Being host of *You Gotta Eat Here!* has afforded me unparalleled opportunity to meet incredible people and feast on their delicious creations. What often don't get told on the show, however, are the tales of the glorious places I've gotten to visit along the way. My conclusion? Yes, we're the True North strong and free. And we're pretty freakin' beautiful, too.

Take the Rocky Mountains, for example. Their rugged beauty is well known, but not to me. At least not until we visited Canmore and Banff, Alberta, back in 2014. Wow! Jagged peaks loom on the horizon even from the airport in Calgary, some 100 kilometres away. But to drive into the Bow Valley and be surrounded by the Rockies is to be in the company of kings.

When it comes to rugged beauty, few Canadian cities rival Whitehorse, Yukon. The town is an extremely cool mix of rustic and modern, where log buildings happily coexist with their steel-and-glass brothers and sisters. But it's the Yukon River (which flows right through town) and the surrounding mountains that give Whitehorse its incomparable beauty.

And no, I'm not just a blockhead who thinks things have to be rugged to be gorgeous. Just outside of Charlottetown, PEI, we drove through a series of rolling fields that were the richest shade of green I've ever seen. Signal Hill—which overlooks the dramatic harbour of St. John's, Newfoundland—is one of the most breathtaking spots I've ever been.

Most Canadians have never heard of Vermilion Bay, Ontario, but if you step outside there on a clear night you'll see a canopy of stars overhead that will make you feel like you're one with the gods.

And if you're a Star Wars buff, Vancouver Island's Cathedral Grove is so much like the forest moon of Endor that I couldn't help riding on Steve's back like Yoda on Luke Skywalker. (Steve is our director of photography. And, yes, I know that happened in *The Empire Strikes Back* and not *Return of the Jedi*. Relax, nerds.) Trees there (mostly Douglas fir) are ancient and can grow to as much as 30 feet (!) in circumference. Insignificant did I feel when we visited, young Padawan.

All this natural beauty explains why we spend so much time stopping to take snapshots. Don't get me wrong, we like taking selfies as much as everybody else. But when you've got scenery like this all around, why bother?

Wait ... is that an Ewok? Maybe not, but Cathedral Grove is out-of-this-world cool, with trees that can grow over 200 feet tall! Damn, I love being Canadian.

For many Canadian performers, crossing over to the south is a step towards the big-time. I felt it when I was a comedian and, truth be told, I felt it as host of *You Gotta Eat Here!*, too. When we filmed those first two special episodes in Chicago and Miami in Season 3, it dawned on both me and the crew that we were evolving, growing up. And that, my friends, was a wonderful feeling.

It's not like the crossover wasn't without a certain amount of anxiety, though. How would the show translate to an American market? Would they be as open and receptive to us as Canadian restaurateurs had been? In the end, the transition was seamless. Everyone we worked with on the other side of the border was as open and accommodating as their Canadian counterparts.

Ego aside, I love travelling to the US for the diversity it offers. Okay, so it's not nearly as massive as Canada (which is pretty freakin' massive!), but the regional diversity still makes it seem like you're sometimes travelling between countries. I mean, do Miami and Chicago *really* have that much in common . . . other than they're both in America?

One thing I have learned about the States, though: The legend of their portions is true—they're *huge!* And that's not just in Texas, people. Most joints are quite happy to set plates in front of you that will leave you gasping for air. But hey, I'm as game as the next guy to pull up my sleeves and get down to business!

AUSTIN, TX

Mi Madre's
Est. 1990
2201 Manor Rd.
Austin, TX 78722
(512) 322-9721
www.mimadresrestaurant.com

· ·

Austin's premier breakfast taco joint has been dishing out Mexican breakfasts for over twenty years, and they've got loads of faithful followers. Two Torres generations are mirrored by two generations of customers: folks who ate there as kids and now bring their own children! Edgar Torres plates up the best breakfast tacos, going through more than 5000 eggs per week and over 3000 tortillas! Grab a taco to go or, better still, a coffee and carnita to stay at Mi Madre's!

Noble Sandwich
Est. 2010
12233 Ranch Rd. 620 N, #105
Austin, TX 78750
(512) 382-6248
www.noblesandwiches.com

· ·

Noble Sandwich's chef and owner, John Bates, is using his high-end culinary chops to elevate everyone's favourite lunchtime classic. Reimagining sandwiches with a start-from-scratch approach, John shares his love for nose-to-tail cooking, giving these sammies a delicious upgrade. Not only do they bake their own bread (from rye to challah), they cure all their meat and pickle all the vegetables, making Noble Sandwiches . . . well, noble.

LOCAL GEMS

Bat Watching at Congress Avenue Bridge

If you're looking for something a little unusual to occupy your evening, look no further than the Congress Avenue Bridge in downtown Austin. Gather on the bridge with hundreds of other onlookers to watch as Mexican free-tailed bats emerge from underneath and set to the skies. Since the bridge's reconstruction in 1980, multitudes of bats have sought shelter in its crevices, making it home to the world's largest urban bat colony. You're sure to be in for an interesting sight, as more than 1.5 million bats circle the skies. Congress Ave., Austin, TX, 78704. www.batcon.org/index.php/our-work/regions/usa-canada/protect-mega -populations/cab-intro.

Broken Spoke

If you're looking to soak in some authentic Texan two-stepping, then the Broken Spoke is the place for you! Experience part of Austin's history by dancing the night away at one of Texas's top dancehalls. Not only does this quintessential dancehall offer you the chance to enjoy live country music, drinks, and food, but it also gives you the opportunity to learn classic dance moves like the two-step, the Cotton-Eyed Joe, and the Western Swing. 3201 Lamar Blvd. S, Austin, TX, 78704. www.brokenspokeaustintx.net.

BOSTON, MA

Saus

Est. 2010
33 Union St.
Boston, MA 02108
(617) 248-8835
www.sausboston.com

. . . .

The Belgians have arrived at Boston's Freedom Trail—and they've brought food. Saus is ahead of the curve with a super-strong fry game that's garnered attention worldwide. Tanya Kropinicki and the team go through an average of 1750 pounds of Idaho Russet potatoes a week! And fries are just one of the Belgian delights found here. Try the golden waffles and frikandellen sandwiches brimming with homemade fillings. Don't forget to say *dank je* when Tanya treats you to Boston's favourite Belgian treats!

LOCAL GEM

The Mapparium

The Mary Baker Eddy Library was created to honour the passions and ideas of its namesake, Mary Baker Eddy, a prominent 19th-century author. Nestled inside this library/museum lies a unique exhibit called the Mapparium: a three-storey stained-glass globe that gives visitors a three-dimensional view of the world in 1935. Cross the 30-foot bridge to step into the middle of the globe and enjoy an audio-visual presentation designed to showcase the way ideas can traverse the globe over time. 200 Massachusetts Ave., Boston, MA, 02115. www.marybakereddylibrary .org/project/mapparium/ 02115.

BUFFALO, NY

Fat Bob's Smokehouse
Est. 1999
41 Virginia Pl.
Buffalo, NY 14202
(716) 887-2971
www.fatbobs.com

. . . .

If you're in Buffalo's historic Allentown and you catch a whiff of hickory, follow your nose, forget your diet, and find a seat! Chef Adam Zimpfer is smokin' all your traditional barbecue fare like brisket and pulled pork, but he's also got some tricks up his sleeve. The Pork Bomb is all kinds of fun on a bun. At Fat Bob's they're always thinking, "What can we smoke next?" The constant smell of meat wafting may have something to do with the answer.

LOCAL GEM

The Buffalo Transportation Pierce-Arrow Museum

If you like classic cars, then this is the place for you. Operating out of Buffalo between 1901 and 1938, the Pierce-Arrow Motor Car Company manufactured motorcycles, bicycles, fire trucks, and, most famously, luxury American automobiles. The Pierce-Arrow Museum is the result of forty-five years' worth of artifact collecting, and the bounty has been been put on display to showcase the company's rich local history. The 20,000-square-foot museum is filled with an eclectic mix of automobiles, bicycles, statues, paintings, and other Pierce-Arrow memorabilia. 263 Michigan Ave., Buffalo, NY, 14203. www.pierce-arrow.com.

CAMBRIDGE, MA

Frank's Steakhouse
Est. 1938
2310 Massachusetts Ave.
North Cambridge, MA 02140
(617) 661-0666
www.frankssteakhouse.com

. . . .

Fancy downtown Boston steakhouses may be the places to see and be seen, but Frank's is where those in the know go for great cuts of meat at amazing prices. Owner George Ravanis has been working at this legendary restaurant since his family took over in 1974, and he's kept the classic charm, quality, and value that Bostonians remember. Try the "Sizzler," a 15-ounce sirloin—for a mere $25 (US). It's no wonder this steak has been a favourite since the restaurant originally opened in 1938.

LOCAL GEM

Modica Way

Amidst all the ivy-coated buildings, university campuses, and historic landmarks, witness some modern street art on Cambridge's "graffiti alley." This free-for-all graffiti wall offers visitors the chance to see something different every time they come. Partially covered by a stained-glass canopy, this alleyway offers a 24-hour art gallery that features both art installed by the city as well as a revolving door of local artists' work. The alleyway has also featured art from several nationally renowned artists over the years. 565–567 Massachusetts Ave., Cambridge, MA, 02139.

CHICAGO, IL

Lou Malnati's
Est. 1971
1120 North State St.
Chicago, IL 60610
(312) 725-7777
www.loumalnatis.com

· · · · · · · · · · · · · · ·

Any Chicagoan will tell you if you're gonna do deep dish, you gotta go where it all started: Lou Malnati's Pizzeria. Seventy years and three generations later, grandson Marc Malnati continues the family tradition. Anyone with this much pizza sauce running through his veins knows a great pizza when he makes it and tastes it. This is one handful of a slice you'd better sit down to enjoy!

Manny's Cafeteria and Delicatessen
Est. 1942
1141 South Jefferson St.
Chicago, IL 60607
(312) 939-2855
www.mannysdeli.com

· · · · · · · · · · · · · · ·

Nobody does deli quite like Manny's Cafeteria and Deli. Four generations of Raskin men have dedicated their lives to crafting mouth-stretching Reubens, pastrami sandwiches, and life-altering Jewish delicacies like golden matzo ball soup. Slide your cafeteria tray down the line—it's a Chicago rite of passage! You might even rub elbows with famous politicians from the nearby Democrat headquarters. Bill Clinton, Rahm Emmanuel, and Barack Obama know that if you want to eat with the people, you gotta eat at Manny's!

LOCAL GEM

Oz Park

Originally created as a means to rejuvenate a neighbourhood, Oz Park has now become an ever-expanding homage to the work of *Wizard of Oz* author L. Frank Baum, who once lived nearby. The park features life-size statues of Dorothy, Toto, Scarecrow, Tin Man, and Cowardly Lion, as well as themed park areas like "Dorothy's Playlot" and "Emerald Gardens." 2021 N. Burling St., Chicago, IL, 60614. www.chicagoparkdistrict.com/parks/Oz-Park.

CLEVELAND, OH

Happy Dog at the Euclid Tavern
Est. 2009
11625 Euclid Ave.
Cleveland, OH 44106
(216) 231-5400
www.happydogcleveland.com

. . . .

A live music institution with a polka night every Tuesday, Cleveland's Euclid Tavern has a storied rock 'n' roll history, but chef Eric Williams is the real rock star. Served over-the-top hot dogs and tater tots, Clevelanders get a little wild with the fifty-plus homemade toppings—try pulled pork, chili, curried peanut butter, and even Froot Loops! So grab a dog and rock 'n' roll with Happy Dog at the Euclid Tavern.

Sweet Moses
Est. 2011
6800 Detroit Ave.
Cleveland, OH 44102
(216) 651-2202
www.sweetmosestreats.com

. . . .

At this 1920s soda shop named after the city's founder, life is simple. It's nothing but sweet dreams and whipped cream here. Watch owner and chef Jeff Moreau whip up old-fashioned chocolate soda floats from scratch with his antique soda machine, or snuggle up in a church pew for sundaes named after Cleveland landmarks. Jeff also serves his sundaes at Progressive Field, home to the Cleveland Indians. In baseball lingo, that's hitting a double!

HIDDEN GEMS

Cleveland Police Museum

Peek inside the world of Cleveland's police force at one of the few remaining law enforcement museums in the United States. The 4000-square-foot museum is home to decades of police memorabilia and paraphernalia. Browse exhibits showcasing the police's role in enforcing Prohibition laws; their K-9, motorcycle, and mounted units; Eliot Ness's work in the city; famous Cleveland crime scenes; and so much more. To top it off, admission is free! Cleveland Police Headquarters, First Floor, 1300 Ontario St., Cleveland, OH, 44113. www.clevelandpolicemuseum.org.

LOCAL GEM

Peabody Hotel: The Duck March

If Graceland isn't your style, you can visit the Peabody Hotel, where arguably the world's most pampered ducks reside. A tradition dating back to the 1930s, a duck march takes place daily. At around 11 each morning the "Duckmaster" leads the ducks from their $200,000 rooftop penthouse to the hotel's lobby, where they waddle their way across a red carpet to the hotel's fountain. The ducks spend their day frolicking in the water until 5 p.m., when they are ceremoniously returned to their posh living quarters. Peabody Hotel, 149 Union Ave., Memphis, TN, 38103. www.peabodymemphis.com/ducks-en.html.

MEMPHIS, TN

Kooky Canuck
Est. 2005
87 South 2nd St.
Memphis, TN 38103
(901) 578-9800
www.kookycanuck.com

· · · · · · · · · · · · · ·

The Kooky Canuck in downtown Memphis delivers some of Canada's food favourites to our friends down south. Canadian-born chef Shawn Danko brings Canuck delicacies like Montreal poutine, Hamilton-inspired maple bread pudding, and Halifax donair to the good ole boys and girls of Memphis, Tennessee. It's not just Canadiana. This place is called "Kooky" for a reason: How about BBQ Egg Rolls or a 4-pound Kookamonga Burger Challenge? Kooky? Sure. Delicious? Definitely.

Payne's Bar-B-Que
Est. 1972
1762 Lamar Ave.
Memphis, TN 38114
(901) 272-1523

· · · · · · · · · · ·

Since 1972, Payne's Bar-B-Que has been serving some of the best barbecue sandwiches Memphis has to offer. From their famous chopped pork to their bone-in ribs on a bun, Ronald Payne uses techniques from old recipes handed down from his dad. He's all about delicious, unpretentious barbecue for a great price. And at Payne's flavour is king: It's the perfect combination of smoky, sour, and sweet that has kept people coming here for the past forty years—and probably for the next forty to come!

MIAMI, FL

11th Street Diner
Est. in Pennsylvania 1948;
in Miami 1992
1065 Washington Ave.
Miami Beach, FL 33139
(305) 534-6373
www.eleventhstreetdiner.com

. . . .

In the heart of Miami's iconic Art Deco District, a 1948 Airstream-style dining car is home to the 11th Street Diner. There, you'll find a retro atmosphere and delicious food inspired by Floridian and South American culture. Chef Jean Lysius's Argentinian skirt steak is garnished with chimichurri, a nod to the thriving South American communities in town. And of course it's not a visit to South Florida without key lime pie for dessert! Every meal comes with a side of Miami history.

El Mago de las Fritas
Est. 1983
5828 Southwest 8th St.
West Miami, FL 33144
(305) 266-8486
www.elmagodelasfritas.com

. . . .

When in Miami, everyone goes to El Mago de las Fritas. It's a super-casual, 100% authentic Cuban diner. Ortelio Cardenas—*el Mago* or "the magician"—is the mastermind behind it all. Even in his late '70s, Ortelio is still in charge of the kitchen, making the patties and his signature sauce for the Fritas himself—he won't share his recipes with anyone. Enjoy the tasty secret that's been delighting Miami for over thirty years.

La Camaronera Seafood Joint and Fish Market
Est. 1966
1952 West Flagler St.
Miami, FL 33135
(305) 642-3322
www.lacamaronera.com

. . . .

When you think of food in Miami, you think of seafood, Cuban flavours, and tradition. One spot serves it all up on a deliciously iconic fried snapper sandwich, the Original Pan Con Minuta. What began as a humble seafood market is now a thriving sit-down restaurant with a full menu of the ocean's finest offerings. *Bienvenidos a La Camaronera!* The name means "the Shrimper" and—owned by the Garcia family for nearly half a century—it's Little Havana's seafood institution!

LOCAL GEMS

Monkey Jungle

Given that monkeys are not indigenous to Florida, you might wonder how a monkey habitat came to be located near Miami. It all started in 1933, when a man with a dream to see monkeys roaming freely about America introduced a small pack of Java monkeys to the area. Now a 30-acre wildlife park, Monkey Jungle gives visitors an opportunity to view monkeys from inside a network of caged pathways that allow the monkeys to roam free— just as they were always meant to. 14805 Southwest 216th St., Miami, FL, 33170. www.monkeyjungle.com.

Wolfsonian-Florida International University (FIU)

Over 120,000 items collected from the height of the Industrial Revolution to the end of the Second World War are on display at the Wolfsonian-Florida International University (FIU). With the intent of showcasing the influence of art and design on the world and how it has progressed over time, the museum offers an eclectic view into industry and technology. Items from around the world are featured so visitors can compare and contrast different cultures and the impression they've left on modern technology. 1001 Washington Ave., Miami Beach, FL, 33139. www.wolfsonian.org.

NASHVILLE, TN, AND SURROUNDING AREA

Edley's Bar-B-Que
Est. 2011
2706 12th Ave. S
Nashville, TN 37204
(615) 953-2951
www.edleysbbq.com

. . . .

Eating at Edley's feels just like hanging out on your best friend's back porch. Decorated with barn board, slightly off-kilter furniture, and a massive back porch where customers enjoy the Nashville heat, this place couldn't be more Southern. And just like your best friend, chef Bret Tuck and the folks at Edley's always make you feel welcome. With giant platters of wings, ribs, and brisket, which holds no state loyalties, Bret's making waves in Nashville's barbecue scene.

The Loveless Cafe
Est. 1951
8400 Tennessee Highway 100
Nashville, TN 37221
(615) 646-9700
www.lovelesscafe.com

. . . .

Twenty miles outside Nashville on Highway 100 is the Loveless Cafe: a world-famous icon for over sixty years. What was once a pit stop is now a destination, with almost half a million visitors a year flocking to try Annie Loveless's original buttermilk biscuits (one of Oprah's favourite things in 2013), Daniel Dillingham's crispy fried chicken, and pit boss George Harvell's smoky barbecue! People come to the Loveless for its laid-back atmosphere and family feeling, as well as the amazing food.

Puckett's

Est. 1998

120 4th Ave. S

Franklin, TN 37064

(615) 794-5527

www.puckettsgro.com

. . . .

The heart and soul of small-town Franklin, Puckett's is a corner-store-turned-restaurant serving up traditional and not-so-traditional Southern food. It has an old-fashioned, homey feel, with lots of barn board, hanging Christmas lights, and country music playing. They have a serious knack for coming up with new versions of classic dishes like the BLT, mac 'n' cheese, and cheesesteak. Try the Redneck Burrito!

LOCAL GEMS

Hatch Show Print

Hatch Show Print got its start in 1879 and quickly rose to legendary status by designing stunning custom posters and handbills. The company has worked with hundreds of celebrities, most commonly country music stars (the shop's in close proximity to the famous Ryman Auditorium). In 2013, the shop was moved in its entirety into the lobby of the Country Music Hall of Fame, where it continues to operate to this day, creating over 150,000 prints each year. 24 5th Ave. S., Nashville, TN, 37203. www.hatchshowprint.com.

The Hermitage Hotel Men's Bathroom

While many buildings and rooms are known for their stunning architecture and decor, a bathroom isn't exactly what you'd think of when you hear the phrase "award-winning design." But let the men's room in Nashville's Hermitage Hotel—operating since 1910—prove you wrong. This stunning art deco–style restroom, with its green-and-black leaded glass tile walls, terrazzo floor, and quaint shoeshine station, is truly one of a kind. And ladies, don't worry: The hotel allows women in to take a look as well. 231 6th Ave. N., Nashville, TN, 37219. www.thehermitagehotel.com.

Country Music Hall of Fame

Biscuits
(Loveless Cafe)

Loveless Cafe

Which Way to the Rhinestone Suit?
That's Tourist, with a Capital "T"

The word *tourist* might have a negative connotation, but the crew and I are quite happy to act like tourists no matter where we end up. Got a giant goose? We'll be there taking photos. Go-kart racing define your town? Hand over the helmets.

Luckily, we've visited a bucket list of towns and cities over the years, which has afforded us ample opportunity to act . . . well . . . touristy. As an added bonus, we have our own private recreation coordinator/tour guide in our sound man Scott. Scott dutifully researches each of our destinations before we get there, then somehow manages to organize a raft of activities to fill our down days.

One of my all-time favourite side trips was to the Country Music Hall of Fame in Nashville, Tennessee, which fed my soft spot for old-time country twang. I couldn't find the "Try On the Rhinestone Suit" exhibit, but sure woulda been in line had I stumbled upon it! We also got to see a Toronto Maple Leafs game while in Nashville, which is another one of our occasional down-day forays. After all, getting tickets for a Leafs home game is virtually impossible, so our only chance is on the road.

In Cleveland we visited the Rock & Roll Hall of Fame, which almost brought the drummer in me to tears. But as much as I loved it, I was a bit disappointed that there weren't more exhibits and information on heavy metal. (What, a guy can't like old-time country *and* metal? C'mon people, it's 2017!)

Memphis, Tennessee, is home to Graceland, and we made sure to get our Elvis fix, especially because we were able to get a behind-the-scenes tour. But what proved most moving in Memphis was the National Civil Rights Museum, which actually incorporates the Lorraine Motel itself, where Martin Luther King Jr. was staying when he was shot. Intense? Absolutely. But eye-opening at the same time, and a place everyone should visit.

In the end, I think travelling is about experiencing what each place—large or small—has to offer. Sure, not everything's as grand as Graceland, but you'll find us there just the same.

Thank ya very much! Yep, that's me and the YGEH! fam, doing our best impersonations of The King himself. Elvis apparently bought his mansion for $100,000 in 1957.

NEW ORLEANS, LA

Dreamy Weenies
Est. 2012
740 North Rampart St.
New Orleans, LA 70116
(504) 872-0157
www.dreamyweenies.com

. . . .

Chicago's got one. New York City's got one. But have you ever heard of a New Orleans–style hot dog? You better believe they've got one, too! We're talking red beans, rice, grits, and a barbecue shrimp sauce that will have you barking for more! Dreamy Weenies has reinvented the dog with a unique twist that absolutely hollahs N'Awlins! Chef Ahmad Shakir even spent three months with a baker perfecting the recipe for his hot dog buns. "The perfect dog is all in the details!" says Shakir.

Katie's
Est. 1984
3701 Iberville St.
New Orleans, LA 70119
(504) 488-6582
www.katiesinmidcity.com

. . . .

You want to eat like a New Orleanian? Then head to Katie's! Katie's isn't known as the quintessential Creole neighbourhood restaurant for nothing. Rebuilt after it was destroyed by Katrina, Katie's offers up traditional New Orleans comfort foods like po' boys and gumbos. The locals are eating it up, packing the joint nightly! Try the Seafood Beignet, a fabulous fritter stuffed with seafood. Big flavours in the Big Easy? Yes, please!

Parkway Bakery & Tavern
Est. 1911/2003
538 Hagan Ave.
New Orleans, LA 70119
(504) 482-3047
www.parkwaypoorboys.com

. . . .

Parkway's been serving up po' boy sandwiches for more than a hundred years! The po' boy was first served as a free meal to striking streetcar workers (nicknamed Poor Boys) during the Great Depression. Today, Parkway gets its delivery of the distinctive New Orleans–style French bread directly from the bakery that invented it—the oldest

in the city! Whether you go for the original roast beef, gravy, and potatoes, or golden fried shrimp, you'll be biting into a scrumptious mouthful of N'Awlins history.

LOCAL GEMS

New Orleans Train Garden

Get an overhead view of New Orleans' past with the 1/22-scale model of the city from the early 19th century, complete with working railroads and streetcars. Nestled in the centre of City Park, this charming attraction will show you a New Orleans you've never seen before. Watch as the train makes its way around the city, stopping at famous locations along the way. The train is in operation on weekends only, and runs between 10:30 a.m. and 4:30 p.m. City Park, 1 Palm Dr., New Orleans, LA, 70124. www.neworleanscitypark.com/in-the-park/train-garden.

The Singing Oak

If you're looking for a place to relax and recharge with some beautiful background ambience, New Orleans has the place for you. Located in the heart of City Park, the Singing Oak, also known as the Chime Tree, has dozens of chimes attached to its branches, all specially tuned to create a peaceful and harmonious symphony of sounds. Sit underneath the tree and let the melodic sounds soothe away your worries as you take a break from the Louisiana heat. City Park, 1 Palm Dr., New Orleans, LA, 70124.

Lardo
Est. 2010
1212 Southeast Hawthorne Blvd.
Portland, OR 97214
(503) 234-7786
www.lardosandwiches.com

. . . .

Go hog-wild at Lardo with Rick Gencarelli's street food—inspired twists on the Italian sandwiches he grew up with. Lardo is named after a cured cut of pork, and it's pretty hard to order something at Lardo without pork in it—and why would you want to? There's a reason Rick goes through 1500 pounds of the stuff a week. Rick serves his sandwiches with a smile and a huge pile of napkins at three Portland-area Lardo locations. The Lardo motto? "Bringing Fat Back!" Oh my!

Shut Up and Eat
Est. 2010
3848 SE Gladstone St.
Portland, OR 97202
(503) 719-6449
www.shutupandeatpdx.com

. . . .

South Philly transplant John Fimmano will tell you that some things in life should be simple. Sandwiches are one of those things. To prove it, he's bringing his mama's real Italian cooking to hungry Portlanders. You'll be at a loss for words when he slams down 11 inches of Italian-style sandwich greatness in front of you. When faced with drippy beef dips, meatball subs with Italian gravy, and the best Philly-style sandwiches in PDX, don't fight the urge . . . just Shut Up and Eat!

Tilt
Est. 2011
1355 Northwest Everett St., #120
Portland, OR 97209
(503) 894-9528
www.tiltitup.com

. . . .

When the steam whistle sounds, nine-to-fivers in the PDX go to Tilt for "Handcrafted Food and Drink Built for the American Workforce"! There you'll find massive burgers to soothe your workday hunger and all-day breakfast sandwiches served on fresh buttermilk biscuits like mama used to make. And what meal would be complete without freshly baked apple pie? You work hard so you deserve it all. So when you punch out at work, punch in at Tilt!

LOCAL GEMS

Mill Ends Park

Known as the world's smallest park, at only two feet wide, located right on the median of the busy Naito Parkway, the Mill Ends Park can be pretty hard to spot. Created by journalist Dick Fagan after he got fed up looking out his office window at a patch of weeds growing in the median, it was dedicated on St. Patrick's Day in 1948 and became the only leprechaun colony west of Ireland. It became an official city park in 1976. Southwest Taylor St. and Southwest Naito Pkwy., Portland, OR, 97204.

Stark's Vacuum Museum

Vacuuming may be an arduous task not many enjoy, but think about just how far the modern vacuum cleaner has come. Stark's Vacuum Museum offers an interesting view into the history of the vacuum cleaner with a range of models from as early as the 1800s. Check out their collection of over 300 vintage vacuum cleaners, including the truly unique two-person Busy-Bee. Take a look at the various machines and rest assured you'll be walking on a spotless floor. 107 Northeast Grand Ave., Portland, OR, 97232. www.starks.com/vacuum-museum.

Rockin' to Vampire Poutine
That's Entertainment!

Being away from home *all the time* means a guy has to develop a certain ability to entertain himself during the down days when we're not shooting. Luckily, I've got the crew to help keep me smiling when I'm feeling lonely. And if that fails, well, there's always Candy Crush.

Video games aside, the crew and I love going to movies whenever we get the chance, though we never know what kind of theatre we'll end up in. Sometimes they're quaint mom-and-pop places where we have to move the chairs when the movie's finished, and other times they're serving us meals in recliners and covering us with blankets. We also went through a hard-core bowling phase where every spare (get it, *spare*?) minute was spent hunting down local lanes.

Water slides are another big form of entertainment for us, largely because our director Jim is a fanatic. Honestly, there are few things on earth that make Jim as happy as walking into a hotel and learning it has a waterslide. The problem is we're often caught without our swim trunks, which necessitates last-minute forays to the nearest shop for a pair. And while nobody's ever been injured during a waterslide outing, I can testify that ill-fitting trunks sometimes shift in uncomfortable ways.

Music is a pretty big part of life on the road, too. The highlight of long drives invariably occurs when an '80s power ballad hits the airwaves (okay, so we might be listening to Whitesnake's "Here I Go Again" as we write this), and nobody *ever* laughs at my singing. Since Scott, Steve, and I all tinker on instruments (me on drums, them on guitar and bass), we'll occasionally rent a rehearsal space and a few instruments, and jam away for a few hours. Hey, we even write our own songs (who wouldn't?). One of our faves is the cult classic "Vampire Poutine."

But it's not all fun and games with the crew. Sometimes I just want to be alone or simply can't resist the siren call of Candy Crush (or whatever other game I happen to be addicted to at the moment). Those are the days I'll just sit in my hotel room, order room service, and stare at a screen or book all day long.

In retrospect, I probably should be doing more productive things during our down time. Hell, I'd likely be fluent in Mandarin by now. But I'm *still* waiting to be invited to a small-town bingo hall for a night of real fun.

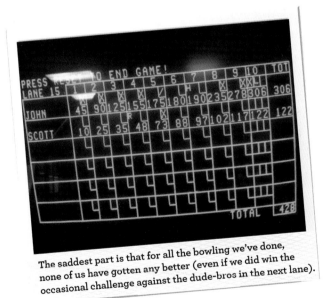

The saddest part is that for all the bowling we've done, none of us have gotten any better (even if we did win the occasional challenge against the dude-bros in the next lane).

SEATTLE, WA

Porkchop & Co.
Est. 2014
5451 Leary Ave.
Seattle, WA 98107
(206) 257-5761
www.eatatporkchop.com
. . . .

Seattle's best brunch is positively pork-filled at deli-inspired Porkchop & Co., where meticulous Paul Osher serves bold dishes like Kimchi Hash and his infamous bone-in pork chop sandwich. Formerly a vegetarian for ten years and a vegan for five, Paul started eating meat again while working at a deli during college. Whatever you order, you'll get a flavourful meal made from scratch with local ingredients and a lotta pork!

Queen Bee Cafe
Est. 2014
2200 East Madison St., Ste. B
Seattle, WA 98112
(206) 757-6314
www.queenbeecafe.com
. . . .

Chef Justin Sledge takes traditional English crumpets and transforms them into brilliant sandwich inventions called "crumpwiches." Whether you crave savoury or sweet, go on, live like royalty and treat yourself at Queen Bee! While you do, you'll also be treating others: in honour of his mother, who passed away from Alzheimer's, owner Dwayne Clarke chooses a new charity each trimester to which *all* Queen Bee profits are donated.

LOCAL GEMS

Spooked in Seattle

Ghosts aren't just for Halloween, and Seattle might just be the place to look for them. Join the real ghost hunters from Spooked in Seattle in the search for paranormal activity around the city. 102 Cherry St., Seattle, WA, 98104. www.spookedinseattle.squarespace.com.

Porkchop & Co.

Queen Bee Cafe

Crumpets (Queen Bee Cafe)

Apple Melt (Porkchop & Co.)

Pork Chop Sandwich (Porkchop & Co.)

TUCSON, AZ

Baja Café
Est. 2014
7002 East Broadway Blvd.
Tucson, AZ 85710
(520) 495-4772
www.bajacafetucson.com

. . . .

American classics made with Southwestern ingredients and a whole lot of love—that's what you'll get from Gerard Meurer at Baja Café. Every weekend Gerard comes up with new over-the-top eggs Benedict and pancake specials. Drawing on ingredients like phyllo pastry and hazelnut pesto hollandaise to wasabi potato and braised short ribs, Gerard's creativity knows no limits. Eating at Baja Café is as much about the experience as it is about the food. Every breakfast at Baja Café is special!

BOCA Tacos y Tequila
Est. 2010
828 East Speedway Blvd.
Tucson, AZ 85719
(520) 777-8134
www.bocatacos.com

. . . .

BOCA is offering the people of Tucson an education in old-school tacos with a twist. Try their bacon-wrapped hot dog tacos or wrap your mitts around the AM: a taco packed with hashbrowns and a fried egg. Chef Maria Mazon invents new salsas daily, using ingredients like strawberries, Mexican chocolate, watermelon, curry, and coconut milk. There's no limit to what goes into a salsa at BACO.

Mother Hubbard's Cafe
Est. 1973
14 West Grant Rd.
Tucson, AZ 85705
(520) 623-7976
www.motherhubbardscafe.com

. . . .

Mother Hubbard's Cafe has been the greasy spoon feeding the people of Tucson for decades, but Kelzi Bartholomaei's made it known for more than just the Early Bird Special. She serves contemporary Native American comfort food like Green Corn Waffles. A meal at Mother Hubbard's may include ingredients like cactus, tequila, varieties of corn, and desert spices. You're guaranteed to leave Mother Hubbard's full. Come see what Kelzi fetches from the cupboard next!

LOCAL GEMS

The Mini Time Machine Museum of Miniatures

Containing over 300 miniature houses, room boxes, and collectibles, the Mini Time Machine Museum of Miniatures provides an interesting view on the world through its three main exhibits: the Enchanted Realm, which features fairy-tale-like scenes and figures; the History Gallery, which contains artifacts from significant eras and includes one of the oldest miniature houses in the US (from 1775); and the Exploring the World exhibit, which showcases miniatures from different cultures around the world. 4455 East Camp Lowell Dr., Tucson, AZ, 85712. www.theminitimemachine.org.

Yikes Toys

Advertised as a "cornucopia for the curious," Yikes Toys features an ever-changing display of items perfect for anyone who likes things a little on the wacky side. Combining fun and science, this toy shop isn't your typical Toys 'R' Us. With products ranging from old-school classics like lunch boxes, lava lamps, and toy robots to creations from local artists and scientists, this toy shop has something for everyone, young or old. 2930 East Broadway Blvd., Tucson, AZ, 85716. www.yikestoys.com.

INTERNATIONAL

Like most people, I find it extremely exciting to leave home and venture out into the great wide world. Yes, I *love* Canada and everything it has to offer. But there's something about going overseas that feels, well, exotic.

Just like when we shot in the US for the first time, going to Europe scared the crap out of me and the crew, mostly because we had no idea what to expect. Sure, our concept had translated well south of the 49th parallel, but that didn't mean it would do the same on another continent.

Well, the good news is that food is universal: In the end, everybody's gotta eat; it's just the shape and size that differs. Learning that—and seeing that the show could still work thousands of mile from home—was very special, indeed.

TV notwithstanding, heading to Europe offered a chance to experience places that many of us had only ever heard about. Ireland was pure magic, from its smiling people to the rolling green fields that reminded me of PEI. The sheer size of London was humbling (hell, I thought *Toronto* was big!), but its out-of-the-way neighbourhoods had a charming hominess that made me want to wander aimlessly for days on end.

But there will always be a special place in this guy's heart for Italy, where my mother and father were born. I'd been there before, but it was different with a few more years under my belt, a bit more knowledge in my head, and a few more dollars in my pocket. Sadly, we never got to visit my parents' hometown, but experiencing Rome and Florence in all their majesty was simply incredible.

Are our countries that different? Sure we are . . . and that's a beautiful thing. But when you speak the common language of food, everybody is family.

The Wisdom of the Doughnut
John's Travel Tips

I may not be the sharpest tool in the shed, but a guy who spends as much time in planes, trains, and automobiles as I do learns a few things. Okay, so we don't spend that much time in trains . . . I just couldn't resist the lure of the movie title.

Mode of transportation notwithstanding, here are some surefire tips to help make any excursion easier.

Invest in a good set of noise-cancelling headphones

This is a big one for me, since they give me the option of talking to my neighbours on the plane or simply zoning out. After all, nothing says "Leave me alone" to your seatmate more than a giant set of headphones wrapped around your cranium.

Travel with antibacterial wipes

Wait, you're *not* a germophobe? Well, you should be. Do you have any idea what's crawling around on that seat? So wipe that baby clean before you park your butt in it for the next few hours. Plus, getting sick away from home is *the worst thing ever*. I'm a big baby at home at the best of times. Being sick on the road means there's nobody around to take care of me, and I hate that.

Don't forget your tablet

Okay, so I'm a quasi-millennial screen junkie . . . at least I recognize it. Whatever. My tablet lets me watch movies, play games, and even create drum beats (*not* always a hit with my seatmates). Sure, you *might* get a great movie selection on the plane or you *might* have a book. But you might not. And then what?

Always be nice to the person checking you in

Why? Because they possess a very powerful super power: the power to upgrade you.

Take a picture of your packed stuff

Okay, so this one may be for the neat freaks in the house, but if you want to make sure you get all your stuff back *into* the same place you got it *out of*, take a picture of it once it's packed. This is especially helpful if you happen to be packing hundreds of pounds of luggage and gear into a couple of vans while filming a travelling TV show.

Most importantly, make sure you have snacks for the ride

Because airplane food sucks. And on long road trips, powdered dough-nuts are always—*always*—a good idea.

No, I didn't need this selfie to remember how to get myself into the elevator. Come to think of it, though, it's not such a bad idea. . . .

DUBLIN, IRELAND

Gallagher's Boxty House
Est. 1990
20-21 Temple Bar
Dublin 2, Ireland
(+353) 1 677 2762
www.boxtyhouse.ie
. . . .

On Dublin's Temple Bar—where pints flow like water—you'll find Gallagher's Boxty House, where chef Pádraic Óg Gallagher puts his creative spin on the traditional boxty (Irish potato pancake). Pádraic's a potato expert and likes to respect tradition, so he uses the very same potatoes Ireland grew before the Irish blight—and he goes through about 50 tons of them a year! You'll do more than raise a fork after tasting Pádraic's boxty pancakes and loaves—you'll raise a glass! *Sláinte mhaith!*

L. Mulligan Grocer
Est. 1790
18 Stoneybatter
Dublin 7, Ireland
(+353) 1 670 9889
www.lmulligangrocer1.weebly.com
. . . .

Part of a neighbourhood built by cow traders, L. Mulligan Grocer has long been the hub of the community—the grocery store, the inn, and even the morgue when it opened in 1790! Chef Seaneen Sullivan's meals are as unforgettable as they are historical. There's nothing like meat and potatoes to cure what ails ya. Seaneen's Scotch eggs are a must. The pork belly with a black pudding mash and beer-spiked desserts wow customers and food critics alike. Pull up a seat in this picturesque, bookshelf-lined pub and enjoy.

Oar House Restaurant
Est. 2003
8 West Pier, Howth
Dublin, Ireland
(+353) 1 839 4562
www.oarhouse.ie
. . . .

For a breath of fresh ocean air—and freshly caught seafood—head to the Oar House, an institution at the foot of Howth's rolling hills and panoramic seaside cliffs. With seafood that comes steamed, sauced, or sautéed, and a view to be remembered, it's no wonder Oar House is so popular. One favourite is chef John Aungier's famous fish pie. You may be on dry land at Oar House, but you'll feel at home by the sea.

LOCAL GEMS

The National Leprechaun Museum

More an interactive experience than a museum, Dublin's National Leprechaun Museum takes you on an immersive experience through time to showcase the history of leprechauns and their relationship with Irish folklore. The unique guided tour lets you recreate experiences and explore Irish history that you'll never encounter anywhere else. The museum offers day tours for all ages and special night tours for adults only. For an intimate view into the world of leprechauns, magic, and Ireland, this is the place to go. Jervis St., Dublin 1, Ireland. www.leprechaunmuseum.ie.

Phoenix Park

Experience nature in the midst of the city when you visit Phoenix Park in Dublin. The park is home to a herd of fallow deer, which have roamed the area freely since their introduction to the habitat in the 1660s. Located just a hop, skip, and a jump away from the bustling urban areas of Dublin, Phoenix Park is home to more than 350 deer. These enchanting wild deer provide the perfect opportunity for a reconnection with nature and wonderful photography. Phoenix Park, Dublin 8, Ireland. www.phoenixpark.ie.

FLORENCE, ITALY

All'Antico Vinaio
Est. 1995
Via dei Neri 74 R
50122 Florence, Italy
(+39) 055 238 2723
www.allanticovinaio.com

. . . .

All'Antico may be tucked away in a little alleyway, but it's on food lovers' radars world wide. Tommaso Mazzanti's sandwiches are the *primo* in Florence and the lineups prove it. Faves include the Favolosa with fennel-spiked Sbriciolona salami and spicy eggplant. All'Antico was named TripAdvisor's Most Reviewed Restaurant in the World in 2014, and has even hosted famous customers like Lenny Kravitz and Ron Howard. The world agrees: You gotta eat here!

Trattoria Mario
Est. 1953
Via Rosina 2 R
50123 Florence, Italy
(+39) 055 218550
www.trattoria-mario.com

. . . .

Four generations of Colzis are behind Florence's famed Trattoria Mario: a no-frills lunch spot where diners sit elbow-to-elbow enjoying Florence's best food. It's been everyone's destination since it opened in 1953, when Romeo Colzi started serving Tuscan classics like ribollita, ossobuco, and hearty beef stew. Now grandson Romeo is running the show—*tutti a tavola* (everyone to the table) for a Florentine dynasty's unforgettable dishes!

Trattoria 4 Leoni
Est. 1995
Via dei Vellutini 1 R
50125 Florence, Italy
(+39) 055 218562
www.4leoni.com
· · · · · · · · · · · ·

Transformed from a post-war wine-and-cheese shop to an elegant trattoria by owner and local football legend Stefano di Puccio, Trattoria 4 Leoni is a beautiful setting for a meal in Florence's bustling Piazza della Passera. Pull up a chair to *mangia* and people-watch under charming white umbrellas, and treat yourself to some Tuscan specialties. Faves include his beefy peposo stew, seasonal homemade pastas loaded with wild black truffles, and mascarpone cheesecake. It's a feast for the mouth and for the eyes!

LOCAL GEM

The Bull of Santa Maria del Fiore

Two stories exist about one of the oddest sculptures in the city. One states that it was designed to honour the animals used during the cathedral's creation, and the other claims that the bull was crafted to spite the husband of a stonemason's lover for putting an end to their torrid affair. The horns of the bull are said to be pointing directly towards where the husband's shop was once located. Whichever story you choose to believe, check out the unique sculpture located on the left side of the cathedral. Piazza del Duomo, 50122, Florence, Italy (over the entrance known as "porta delle mandorle"). www.ilgrandemuseodelduomo.it/monumenti/1-cattedrale.

Flavio al Velavevodetto
Est. 2007
Via di Monte Testaccio 97
00153 Rome, Italy
(+39) 06 5744194
www.ristorantevelavevodetto.it

· ·

Flavio al Velavevodetto is a place of overwhelming beauty—both on and off the plate. At this tucked-away food lover's paradise nestled into Monte dei Cocci (an artificial hill made of ancient terracotta fragments), you'll feel like you're dining among ruins. Here you'll find Flavio de Maio toiling over deeply traditional dishes, hand-rolling and cutting his pastas with a *chitarra*. Enjoy the slow-braised oxtail and the tiramisu that's whipped up light as air. This might just be Rome's top trattoria!

La Gatta Mangiona
Est. 1999
Via Federico Ozanam 30-32
00152 Rome, Italy
(+39) 06 534 6702
www.lagattamangiona.com

· · · · · · · · · · · · · · · · · · · ·

This charming spot is run by the quirky Giancarlo Casa. Unlike most restaurateurs in this stray cat–filled city, Giancarlo is fond of Rome's frisky felines, who wander the streets looking for food and causing mischief. He named his restaurant "the Greedy Cat" after a fairy tale his wife used to read to his kids. Giancarlo is famous for his traditional pastas, crispy pizzas, and Italian sweets. If you dream of eating tiramisu alfresco on a bustling Roman patio, this is the place for you!

Tonda
Est. 2011
Via Valle Corteno 31
00141 Rome, Italy
(+39) 06 818 0960

· · · · · · · · · · · ·

What could be more romantic than a rose from one of Rome's best pizza guys? We're talking about chef Stefano Callegari's famous *Rosettone*: a flower-shaped bread he presses and bakes in the oven. The petals puff up to form perfect little pockets to be stuffed with yummy meats, cheeses, and vegetables. For a truly *esperienza fantastica*, head to Tonda in the vibrant neighbourhood of Montesacro. It's more than a pizzeria . . . it's a lifestyle.

LOCAL GEMS

Gianicolo Belvedere Puppet Show

A tradition among Roman locals, the puppet show at Gianicolo Belvedere offers a fun midday activity for the whole family. Whether young or young at heart, everyone will enjoy this delightful Italian entertainment. Featuring the puppet Pulcinella, these half-hour productions, usually offered on Sundays, are put on at an open-air puppet theatre. Call the Teatrino di Pulcinella al Gianicolo directly as show times can vary depending on the weather and the amount of people in attendance. Viale del Gianicolo, Old Town Rome, Italy, (+39) 06 582 7767.

Gruppo Storico Romano:
Learn to Be a Gladiator

Adults and children alike can learn what it takes to become a true Roman gladiator. Open year-round, the *Gruppo Storico Romano* (Gladiator School Rome) gives two-hour weaponry lessons where you can dress up like a real gladiator— helmet, sword, and all! Sign up for authentic training in all its gruelling glory and use your skills to take part in a final duel. Lessons begin at 9 a.m. every day, with the final class starting at 7 p.m. Via Appia Antica 18, 00179, Rome, Italy. www.explore-italian -culture.com/gladiator-school.html.

LONDON, UK

The Princess Victoria

Est. 2011
217 Uxbridge Rd.
London, UK W12 9DH
(+44) 20 8749 5886
www.princessvictoria.co.uk

. . . .

Every week, Brits head to their local pub for Sunday roast, and the Princess Victoria is home to one of London's best. It was recently named London County's Dining Pub of the Year! Tradition reigns at this restored Victorian gin palace, where chef Matt Robinson, a former Gordon Ramsay protégé, serves sumptuous roast beef, lamb, or pork with traditional sides and Yorkshire pudding. For dessert, you'd be daft not to try Matt's sticky toffee pudding. Get your Sunday sorted right here.

Roti Chai

Est. 2011
3 Portman Mews S
London, UK W1H 6HS
(+44) 20 7408 0101
www.rotichai.com

. . . .

Curry is as quintessential to British cuisine as classic fish and chips. In fact, many now consider it to be *the* national dish! You'll find truly exceptional Indian fare at Roti Chai in the Mayfair district, nestled behind legendary London department store Selfridge's. Chef Karan Kashyap is turning heads with award-winning butter chicken, tandoor-cooked meats, and North Indian street food. Karan's curries are fit for a royal, but they're yours for affordable prices!

The Mayfair Chippy
Est. 2014
14 North Audley St.
London, UK W1K 6WE
(+44) 20 7741 2233
www.mayfairchippy.com

. . . .

Fish and chips are as British as the Queen herself. And what better place to dine on a national dish than at Mayfair Chippy: London's only Michelin-listed fish-and-chip shop! It's so popular that chef Pete Taylor goes through over 2800 pounds of fish a week. The dish is just one of many delicious UK classics on the menu, though. Feast on shepherd's pie at this can't-miss London dining destination!

LOCAL GEMS

The Lullaby Factory

Designed to brighten up an awkward and small space left between the Great Ormond Street Hospital for children and a newer modern glass building next door, the Lullaby Factory was installed in 2012. It is crafted out of a fantastical-looking collection of pipes and horns, which play music that can be heard from special "listening pipes" inside the hospital. The music is also broadcast on a radio frequency so the young patients in the wards can listen as well. Attached to the side of the brick building, the installation spans ten storeys and looks like it came from a children's storybook. Great Ormond Street Hospital, Great Ormond St., London, UK, WC1N 3JH. www.studioweave.com/projects/detail/lullaby-factory.

The Mail Rail

Throughout the 20th century this two-track tunnel ran under the city and served as a kind of early-days instant messaging system for London's Royal Mail operations. The service connected eight different postal offices from Paddington to Whitechapel, and was used to quickly transport mail between locations. The system continued to be in use until 2003, but with only three of the original post offices still in operation along the route, the upkeep became too costly and it was shut down. The Postal Museum, Phoenix Place, London, UK, WC1X 0DA. www.postalmuseum.org.

Acknowledgements

I've often said that I have the greatest job in the world, and I've meant it every time. In addition to eating and travelling for a living, I also get to work with some of the best people I've ever met . . . and this book is no exception.

My professional thanks always begin with my manager Lorne Perlmuter at Diamondfield Entertainment. The Lone Eagle Entertainment team has also been behind me from the start; I owe a lot to the dedication of Michael Geddes and Sheldon Teicher, though it certainly does not end with them. Thanks also to producers Rachel Horvath, Steven Mitchell, and Sarah Nixey, as well as to the hard-working research crew in the office: Sarah Hewitt, Dila Velazquez, Bridget Lee, Margie Shields, and Gabriela Skubincan.

Life on the road can be tough, but it's a heck of a lot easier when you're with family. And that's just what Jim Morrison, Sarah Cutts, Scott Chappel, Steve Lindsay, Josh Henderson, and Naela Choudhary have become to me. You guys are the best.

Special thanks to my brother and co-writer Mike Vlessides; thanks for making work fun, pal. And the good people at HarperCollins—especially Brad Wilson—are masters at keeping all our wacky personalities in line.

Then there's my family, without whom none of this would be possible. That starts with my mom, Diana, as well as my sisters, Marta and Rose, and their wonderful families. But if it starts with my extended family, it ends my wife, Shawne, and my daughters, Ruby and Claire. I carry my love for you guys with me into every city and restaurant I visit. You are always with me, no matter how far away I may be.

Finally, this book is for all those with a dream to travel, to live, and (most importantly!) to eat.

—John Catucci

* * *

Well, this is becoming quite a habit, isn't it?

This book marks the third time I've had the distinct privilege of working with a group of ridiculously talented and strikingly committed people, and I'm a better man for it. Though a deviation from our first two iterations, *You Gotta Go Here!* was no less a gas to put together.

Of the myriad personalities whose efforts are woven through the pages of the book, none played a more integral role than Brad Wilson at Harper-Collins and Sheldon Teicher at Lone Eagle Entertainment. Brad is as fine an editor as he is a person (and he's damn fine at both), and Sheldon's ability to coordinate personalities—even the occasional outburst from frustrated writers—is uncanny.

Like *You Gotta Eat Here!* itself, *You Gotta Go Here!* would be nothing without the seemingly boundless talents of my friend John Catucci. I'll share arancini with you anywhere, pal!

As for me, well, I would be nothing without my Caroline Elizabeth. I'll love you even when we're ghosts.

—Michael Vlessides

* * *

This book is all about great food, wonderful new friends, and finding new adventures on the road.

It all starts with our TV series *You Gotta Eat Here!* We shot the demo for the show at Haugen's BBQ in 2010, hoping that John Catucci's amazing wit and warmth might tip the balance and get us a show order from Food Network Canada. He did it. John hit it out of the park from the very first shooting day—and so our journey began.

What a trip! We never dreamed that it would lead to a TV series that boasts five seasons and 150 episodes, has won the Best Lifestyle Series at the Canadian Screen Awards (twice), and is seen around the world. Sorry for the humble bragging, but we are so very proud of the show.

We want to acknowledge and thank the folks at Food Network Canada who got us started down this path and helped us stay the course along the way: Christine Shipton, Emily Morgan, Leslie Merklinger, Holly Gillanders, Lisa Godfrey, Krista Look, Lynne Carter, and Larissa Laycock.

John is the heartbeat of the show, but so many people made important contributions to the success of the series. We have had some great crew over the seasons: directors Jim Morrison and Naela Choudhary, along with Steve Lindsay, Sarah Cutts, Scott Chappel, Josh Henderson, Monique Douek, Richard Hughes, Reuben Denty, and many others. Also, the production team in Toronto, as led by Rachel Horvath and Steven Mitchell: Bridget Lee, Sarah Nixey, Dila Velazquez, Sarah Hewitt, Lauren Greenway,

Deanne Marsh, Rachel Wagner, Margie Shields, Gabi Skubincan, Katie Pitt, Morgan Leech, and all the other exceptional staff. Kudos also to the post-production team of Ross Wilson, Paul Mitchell, Krysia Szyszlo, Dawn Bolsby, Jarrid Dudley, Sarah Peddie, Ryan Edwards, and the rest of the post team. Without you, the series would not have been the joyful experience that it was. Thank you!

We also owe a great debt of thanks to all the restaurants across Canada, the United States, and beyond that allowed us to visit and showcase their great food and great people. We are always amazed by your creativity and passion. We are happy to have had the opportunity to tell your stories and spread the good word.

Kudos also to our great collaborators on this third *You Gotta Eat Here!* book: Mike Vlessides, Brad Wilson, Shannon Whibbs, and the whole team at HarperCollins.

Finally, and most of all, thanks to the fans who watch the show, buy the books, and send us their love and their tips for the next great spot. You inspire us to do our best work. We hope this book inspires you to go out and start your own next great food adventure . . . whether it be across the country, down the street, or in your own kitchen. Enjoy!

—Michael Geddes and Sheldon Teicher,
Lone Eagle Entertainment Ltd.

Photo Credits

All photographs by Josh Henderson except for the following:

Front cover (road): iStock.com/SensorSpot
Front cover (John): Geoff George
Back cover: Dinosaur photo by istock.com/mikeuk

p. ii	Geoff George
p. viii	courtesy of John Catucci
p. 6	iStock.com/ronniechua
p. 11	iStock.com/zennie (middle)
p. 21	iStock.com/mikeuk
p.22–23	iStock.com/brytta
p. 25	Geoff George
p. 27	iStock.com/SolomonCrowe
p. 35	creative commons/Leah Bignell
p. 36	creative commons/Luigi Mengato (right)
p. 37	iStock.com/Murphy_Shewchuk
p. 38	iStock.com/laughingmango
p. 41	500px/Scott Prokop
p. 42	Wikimedia/Canoe1967
p. 43	creative commons/DebMacFadden
p. 45	courtesy of John Catucci
p. 46	courtesy of Wild Play (right)
p. 47	iStock.com/Morlaya
p. 52–53	500px/Jeff Whyte
p. 55	iStock.com/Elenathewise
p. 57	Geoff George
p.73	500px/Michael Gabelman
p. 81	iStock.com/CarrieColePhotography
p. 83	500px/Linda Enkema
p. 87	iStock.com/justinecottonphotography
p. 95	courtesy of Scenic Caves Nature Adventures

YOU GOTTA GO HERE!
RESTAURANT CHECKLIST

WESTERN CANADA

BURNABY, BC, AND SURROUNDING AREA
❏ Fraser Park Restaurant
Est. 1996
4663 Byrne Rd., #103
Burnaby, BC V5J 3H6
(604) 433-7605
www.fraserparkrestaurant.com

❏ Hilltop Diner
Est. 1942
23904 Fraser Highway
Langley, BC V2Z 2K8
(604) 514-9424

CALGARY, AB
❏ Beer Revolution
Est. 2011
1080 8th St. SW
Calgary, AB T2R 0J3
(403) 264-2739
www.beerrevolution.ca

❏ Big Fish
Est. 2004
1112 Edmonton Trail NE
Calgary, AB T2E 3K4
(403) 277-3403
www.big-fish.ca

❏ Big T's BBQ & Smokehouse
Est. 2004
2138 Crowchild Trail NW
Calgary, AB T2M 3Y7
(403) 284-5959
www.bigtsbbq.com

❏ Boogie's Burgers
Est. 1969
908A Edmonton Trail NE
Calgary, AB T2E 3K1
(403) 230-7070
www.boogiesburgers.com

❏ Bookers BBQ Grill and Crab Shack
Est. 1998
316 3rd St. SE, #10
Calgary, AB T2G 2S4
(403) 264-6419
www.bookersbbq.com

❏ The Bro'kin Yolk
Est. 2015
12580 Symons Valley Rd. NW, #130
Calgary, AB T3P 0A3
(587) 317-5743
www.brokinyolk.ca

❏ Diner Deluxe
Est. 2001
804 Edmonton Trail NE
Calgary, AB T2E 3J6
(403) 276-5499
www.dinerdeluxe.com

❏ The Fine Diner Bistro
Est. 2012
1420 9th Ave. SE, #4
Calgary, AB T2G 0T5
(403) 234-8885
www.finedinerbistro.ca

❏ Grumans Delicatessen
Est. 2012
230 11th Ave. SE
Calgary, AB T2G 0X8
(403) 261-9003
www.grumans.ca

❏ Holy Grill
Est. 2003
827 10th Ave. SW
Calgary, AB T2R 0A9
(403) 261-9759
www.holygrill.ca

❏ Jelly Modern Doughnuts
Est. 2011
1414 8th St. SW, #100
Calgary, AB T2R 1J6
(403) 453-2053
www.jellymoderndoughnuts.com

❏ Naina's Kitchen
Est. 2010
121 17th Ave. SE
Calgary, AB T2G 1H3
(403) 263-6355
www.nainaskitchen.com

❏ Oak Tree Tavern
Est. 2011
124B 10th St. NW
Calgary, AB T2N 1V3
(403) 270-3347
www.oaktreetavern.ca

❏ The Palomino Smokehouse
Est. 2005
109 7th Ave. SW
Calgary, AB T2P 0W5
(403) 532-1911
www.thepalomino.ca

❏ Pfanntastic Pannenkoek Haus
Est. 1997
2439 54th Ave. SW
Calgary, AB T3E 1M4
(403) 243-7757
www.dutchpancakes.ca

❏ Pig & Duke
Est. 2012
503 4th Ave. SW
Calgary, AB T2P 0J7
(403) 452-0539
www.pigandduke.ca

❏ Tubby Dog
Est. 2005
1022 17th Ave. SW
Calgary, AB T2T 0A5
(403) 244-0694
www.tubbydog.com

❏ UNA Pizza & Wine
Est. 2010
618 17th Ave. SW
Calgary, AB T2S 0B4
(403) 453-1183
www.unapizzeria.com/calgary

CANMORE AND BANFF, AB
❏ The Bear Street Tavern
Est. 2006
211 Bear St.
Banff, AB T1L 1A1
(403) 762-2021
www.bearstreettavern.ca

❏ The Crazyweed Kitchen
Est. 1997
1600 Railway Ave.
Canmore, AB T1W 1P6
(403) 609-2530
www.crazyweed.ca

EDMONTON, AB
❏ Battista's Calzone Co.
Est. 2010
11745 84th St. NW
Edmonton, AB T5B 3C2
(780) 758-1808
www.battistacalzone.com

❏ The Dish Bistro and the
   Runaway Spoon
Est. 1996
12417 Stony Plain Rd. NW
Edmonton, AB T5N 3N3
(780) 488-6641
www.thedishandspoon.com

❏ Highlevel Diner
Est. 1982
10912 88th Ave. NW
Edmonton, AB T6G 0Z1
(780) 433-0993
www.highleveldiner.com

❏ Louisiana Purchase
Est. 1989
10320 111th St. NW
Edmonton, AB T5K 1M9
(780) 420-6779
www.louisianapurchase.ca

❏ MEAT
Est. 2014
8216 104th St. NW
Edmonton, AB T6E 4E6
(587) 520-6338
www.meatfordinner.com

❏ Rostizado
Est. 2014
10359 104th St., #102
Edmonton, AB T5J 1B9
(706) 761-0911
www.rostizado.com

❏ Sloppy Hoggs Roed Hus
Est. 2012
9563A 118th Ave.
Edmonton, AB T5G 0N9
(780) 477-2408
www.sloppyhoggsbbq.com

❏ Soda Jerks Burgers & Bottles
Est. 2011
16616 95th St.
Edmonton, AB T5Z 3L2
(587) 521-9311
www.sodajerks.net

❏ Sofra
Est. 2006
10345 106th St. NW
Edmonton, AB T5J 0J2
(780) 423-3044

❏ Sugarbowl
Est. 1942
10922 88th Ave.
Edmonton, AB T6G 0Z1
(780) 433-8369
www.thesugarbowl.org

❏ Tres Carnales Taquería
Est. 2011
10119 100A St. NW
Edmonton, AB T5J 0R5
(780) 429-0911
www.trescarnales.com

❏ Urban Diner
Est. 2004
12427 102th Ave. NW
Edmonton, AB T5N 0M2
(780) 488-7274
www.urbandiner.com

GIBSONS, BC
❏ Smitty's Oyster House
Est. 2007
643 School Road Wharf
Lower Gibsons, BC V0N 1V0
(604) 886-4665
www.smittysoysterhouse.com

JASPER, AB
❏ Downstream Lounge
Est. 2008
620 Connaught Dr.
Jasper, AB T0E 1E0
(780) 852-9449
www.downstreamjasper.ca

KAMLOOPS, BC
❏ Fiesta Mexicana
Est. 2011
793 Notre Dame Dr.
Kamloops, BC V2C 5N8
(250) 374-3960
www.fiestamexicana.ca

KELOWNA, BC, AND SURROUNDING AREA
❏ The Jammery
Est. 2000
8038 Highway 97 N
Kelowna, BC V4V 1T3
(250) 766-1139
www.jammery.com

❏ Kekuli Café
Est. 2009
3041 Louie Dr., #505
Westbank, BC V4T 3E2
(250) 768-3555
www.kekulicafe.com

LETHBRIDGE, AB, AND SURROUNDING AREA
❏ Chuckwagon Cafe & Cattle Co.
Est. 1973
105 Sunset Blvd.
Turner Valley, AB T0L 2A0
(403) 933-0003
www.chuckwagoncafe.ca

❏ Two Guys and a Pizza Place
Est. 2002
316 11th St. S
Lethbridge, AB T1J 2N8
(403) 331-2222
www.twoguyspizza.ca

MOOSE JAW, SK
❏ Deja Vu Cafe
Est. 2007
16 High St. E
Moose Jaw, SK S6H 0B7
(306) 692-6066
www.dejavucafe.ca

NANAIMO, BC, AND SURROUNDING AREA
❏ Smokin' George's BBQ
Est. 2010
4131 Mostar Rd., #5
Nanaimo, BC V9T 6A6
(250) 585-2258
www.smokingeorgesbbq.com

REGINA, SK
❏ Fresh & Sweet
Est. 2009
2500 Victoria Ave.
Regina, SK S4P 3X2
(306) 751-2233
www.valleygirlscatering.ca/index.php
/menu/freshandsweet

SALMON ARM, BC
❏ Shuswap Pie Company
Est. 2008
331A Alexander St. NE
Salmon Arm, BC V1E 4H7
(250) 832-7992
www.shuswappiecompany.ca

SASKATOON, SK
❏ Bon Temps Café
Est. 2013
223 2nd Ave. S
Saskatoon, SK S7K 1K8
(306) 242-6617
www.bontempscafe.ca

❏ EE Burritos
Est. 2003
705 Central Ave.
Saskatoon, SK S7N 2S4
(306) 343-6264
www.eeburritossaskatoon.com

❏ Homestead Ice Cream
Est. 1978
822 Victoria Ave.
Saskatoon, SK S7N 0Z4
(306) 653-5588
www.homesteadicecream.ca

❏ Prairie Harvest Café
Est. 2012
2917 Early Dr.
Saskatoon, SK S7H 3K5
(306) 242-2928
www.prairieharvestcafe.com

TOFINO, BC
❏ Wildside Grill
Est. 2008
1180 Pacific Rim Highway
Tofino, BC V0R 2Z0
(250) 725-9453
www.wildsidegrill.com

VANCOUVER, BC
❏ The American Cheesesteak Co.
Est. 2011
781 Davie St.
Vancouver, BC V6Z 2S7
(604) 681-0130
www.americancheesesteak.com

❏ Argo Café
Est. 1954
1836 Ontario St.
Vancouver, BC V5T 2W6
(60) 876-3620
www.argocafe.ca

❏ **Belgian Fries**
Est. 1999
1885 Commercial Dr.
Vancouver, BC V5N 4A6
604-253-4220

❏ **Buckstop**
Est. 2013
833 Denman St.
Vancouver, BC V6G 2L7
(604) 428-2528
www.buckstop.ca

❏ **Calabash Caribbean Bistro**
Est. 2010
428 Carrall St.
Vancouver, BC V6B 2J7
(604) 568-5882
www.calabashbistro.com

❏ **Campagnolo Roma**
Est. 2011
2297 Hastings St. E
Vancouver, BC V5L 1V3
(604) 569-0456
www.campagnoloroma.com

❏ **Cannibal Cafe**
Est. 2012
1818 Commercial Dr.
Vancouver, BC V5N 4A5
(604) 558-4199
www.cannibalcafe.ca

❏ **Cartems Donuterie**
Est. 2011
534 West Pender St.
Vancouver, BC V6B 1V3
(778) 708-0996
www.cartems.com

❏ **Chewies Steam & Oyster Bar**
Est. 2011
2201 West 1st Ave.
Vancouver, BC V6K 3E6
(604) 558-4448
www.chewies.ca

❏ **DD Mau**
Est. 2012
1239 Pacific Blvd.
Vancouver, BC V6B 5Z5
(604) 684-4446
www.ddmau.ca

❏ **Deacon's Corner**
Est. 2009
3189 West Broadway
Vancouver, BC V6K 2H2
(778) 379-3727
www.deaconscorner.ca

❏ **El Camino's**
Est. 2010
3250 Main St.
Vancouver, BC V5V 3M5
(604) 875-6246
www.elcaminos.ca

❏ **La Mezcaleria**
Est. 2013
1622 Commercial Dr.
Vancouver, BC V5L 3Y4
(604) 559-8226
www.lamezcaleria.ca

❏ **La Taqueria Pinche Taco Shop**
Est. 2009
322 West Hastings St.
Vancouver, BC V6B 1K6
(604) 568-4406
www.lataqueria.ca

❏ **Lucy's Eastside Diner**
Est. 2010
2708 Main St.
Vancouver, BC V5T 3E8
(604) 568-1550

❏ **Meet on Main**
Est. 2014
4288 Main St.
Vancouver, BC V5V 3P9
(604) 877-1292
www.meetonmain.com

☐ **Neighbour's Restaurant**
Est. 1982
6493 Victoria Dr.
Vancouver, BC V5P 3X5
(604) 327-1456
www.neighboursrestaurant.ca

☐ **Nuba**
Est. 2003
146 East 3rd Ave.
Vancouver, BC V5T 1C8
(604) 568-6727
www.nuba.ca

☐ **Panaderia Latina Bakery**
Est. 2004
4906 Joyce St.
Vancouver, BC V5R 4G6
(604) 439-1414

☐ **Rangoli**
Est. 2004
1480 West 11th Ave.
Vancouver, BC V6H 3H8
(604) 736-5711
www.vijsrangoli.ca

☐ **The Reef Restaurant**
Est. 1999
4172 Main St.
Vancouver, BC V5V 3P7
(604) 874-5375
www.thereefrestaurant.com

☐ **Romer's Burger Bar**
Est. 2010
1873 West 4th Ave.
Vancouver, BC V6J 1M4
(604) 732-9545
www.romersburgerbar.com

☐ **Scandilicious**
Est. 2012
25 Victoria Dr.
Vancouver, BC V5L 2T6
(604) 877-2277
www.scandilicious.com

☐ **Slickity Jim's Chat & Chew**
Est. 1997
3475 Main St.
Vancouver, BC V5V 3M9
(604) 873-6760
www.slickityjims.com

☐ **The Tomahawk**
Est. 1926
1550 Philip Avenue
North Vancouver, BC V7P 2V8
(604) 988-2612
www.tomahawkrestaurant.com

☐ **Topanga Café**
Est. 1978
2904 West 4th Ave.
Vancouver, BC V6K 4A9
www.topangacafe.com

☐ **Via Tevere Pizzeria**
Est. 2012
1190 Victoria Dr.
Vancouver, BC V5L 4G5
(604) 336-1803
www.viateverepizzeria.com

☐ **The Wallflower Modern Diner**
Est. 2009
2420 Main St.
Vancouver, BC V5T 3E2
(604) 568-7554
www.thewallflowermoderndiner.com

☐ **Yolk's**
Est. 2013
1298 East Hastings St.
Vancouver, BC V6A 1S6
(604) 428-9655
www.yolks.ca

VICTORIA, BC
☐ **Bin 4 Burger Lounge**
Est. 2011
716 Goldstream Ave., #102
Langford, BC V9B 2X3
(778) 265-5464
www.bin4burgerlounge.com

❏ Ferris' Oyster Bar
Est. 1991
536 Yates St.
Victoria, BC V8W 1K8
(250) 360-1824
www.ferrisoysterbar.com

❏ Floyd's Diner
Est. 2006
866 Yates St.
Victoria, BC V8W 1L8
(250) 381-5114
www.floydsdiner.ca

❏ FOO Asian Street Food
Est. 2009
769 Yates St.
Victoria, BC V8W 1L6
(250) 383-3111
www.foofood.ca

❏ Jam Café
Est. 2012
542 Herald St.
Victoria, BC V8W 1S5
(778) 440-4489
www.jamcafes.com/victoria

❏ John's Place Restaurant
Est. 1984
723 Pandora Ave.
Victoria, BC V8W 1N9
(250) 389-0711
www.johnsplace.ca

❏ Pagliacci's
Est. 1979
1011 Broad St.
Victoria, BC V8W 2A1
(250) 386-1662
www.pagliaccis.ca

❏ Pig BBQ Joint
Est. 2007
1325 Blanshard St.
Victoria, BC V8W 3S2
(250) 590-5193
www.pigbbqjoint.com

❏ The Pink Bicycle
Est. 2007
1008 Blanshard St.
Victoria, BC V8W 2H5
(250) 384-1008
www.pinkbicycleburger.com

❏ ReBar Modern Food
Est. 1988
50 Bastion Sq.
Victoria, BC V8W 1J2
(250) 361-9223

❏ Shine Café
Est. 2004
1548 Fort St.
Victoria, BC V8S 5J2
(250) 595-2133
www.shinecafe.ca

❏ Tibetan Kitchen Café
Est. 2008
680 Broughton St.
Victoria, BC V8W 2C9
(250) 383-5664
www.tibetankitchen.com

❏ The Village Restaurant
Est. 2007
2518 Estevan Ave.
Victoria, BC V8R 2S7
(250) 592-8311
www.thevillagerestaurant.ca

WINNIPEG, MB, AND SURROUNDING AREA
❏ Bistro Dansk Restaurant
Est. 1977
63 Sherbrook St.
Winnipeg, MB R3C 2B2
(204) 775-5662
www.bistrodansk.com

❏ Boon Burger Café
Est. 2010
79 Sherbrook St.
Winnipeg, MB R3C 2B2
(204) 415-1391
www.boonburger.ca

Kawaii Crepe
Est. 2009
99 Osborne St., #201
Winnipeg, MB R3L 2R4
(204) 415-2833
www.kawaiicrepe.ca

Marion Street Eatery
Est. 2014
393 Marion St.
Winnipeg, MB R2H 0V4
(204) 233-2843
www.marionstreeteatery.com

NuBurger
Est. 2012
472 Stradbrook Ave.
Winnipeg, MB R3L 0J9
(204) 888-1001
www.ilovenuburger.com

Red Top Drive-Inn Restaurant
Est. 1960
219 St. Mary's Rd.
Winnipeg, MB R2H 1J2
(204) 233-7943
www.redtopdriveinn.com

Summit Café
Est. 2013
23 Main St.
Stony Mountain, MB R0C 3A0
(204) 344-0205
www.summitcafe.ca

The Tallest Poppy
Est. 2007
103 Sherbrook St.
Winnipeg, MB R3B 1E1
(204) 219-8777
www.thetallestpoppy.com

CENTRAL CANADA

COLLINGWOOD, ON
The Iron Skillet
Est. 1989
20 Balsam St., #2
Collingwood, ON L9Y 4H7
(705) 444-5804
www.theironskillet.ca

The Smoke
Est. 2012
498 First St.
Collingwood, ON L9Y 3J2
(705) 293-5522
www.thesmoke.ca

GATINEAU, QC
Edgar
Est. 2010
60 rue Bégin
Gatineau, QC J9A 1C8
(819) 205-1110
www.chezedgar.ca

GUELPH, ON
Baker Street Station
Est. 2011
76 Baker St.
Guelph, ON N1H 4G1
(519) 265-7960
www.bakerstreetstation.ca

HAMILTON, ON, AND SURROUNDING AREA
Black Forest Inn
Est. 1967
255 King St. E
Hamilton, ON L8N 1B9
(905) 528-3538
www.blackforestinn.ca

Burger Barn
Est. 2011
3000 Fourth Line
Ohsweken, Six Nations of the Grand
River Reserve, ON N0A 1M0
(519) 445-0088
www.burgerbarn.ca

The Burnt Tongue
Est. 2013
10 Cannon St. E
Hamilton, ON L8L 1Z5
(905) 536-1146
www.theburnttongue.com

Chicago Style Pizza Shack
Est. 1975
534 Upper Sherman Ave.
Hamilton, ON L8V 3M1
(905) 575-8800

Culantro
Est. 2013
537 Main St. E
Hamilton, ON, L8M 1H9
(905) 777-0060
www.culantro.ca

The Harbour Diner
Est. 2008
486 James St. N
Hamilton, ON L8L 1J1
(905) 523-7373
www.harbourdiner.com

Jack and Lois
Est. 2012
301 James St. N
Hamilton, ON L8R 2L4
(289) 389-5647
www.jackandlois.com

The Ship
Est. 2009
23 Augusta St.
Hamilton, ON L8N 1P2
(905) 526-0792
www.theship.ca

HUNTSVILLE, ON
That Little Place by the Lights
Est. 2009
76 Main St. E
Huntsville, ON P1H 2C7
(705) 789-2536
www.thatlittleplacebythelights.ca

**KAWARTHA LAKES, ON, AND
SURROUNDING AREA**
The Riverside Inn Restaurant
Est. 2011
7497 Highway 35
Norland, ON K0M2L0
(705) 454-1045
www.riverside-inn.ca

KINGSTON, ON
Dianne's
Est. 2013
195 Ontario St.
Kingston, ON K7L 2Y7
(613) 507-3474
www.dianneskingston.com

Geneva Crepe Bistro
Est. 2010
297 Princess St.
Kingston, ON K7L 1B4
(613) 507-0297
www.genevacrepecafe.com

Harper's Burger Bar
Est. 2010
93 Princess St.
Kingston, ON K7L 1A6
(613) 507-3663
www.harpersburgerbar.com

MLTDWN
Est. 2012
292 Princess St.
Kingston, ON K7L 1B5
(613) 766-1881
www.mltdwn.com

KITCHENER-WATERLOO, ON
Jane Bond
Est. 1995
5 Princess St.
Waterloo, ON N2J 2H5
(519) 886-1689
www.janebond.ca

The Lancaster Smokehouse
Est. 2011
574 Lancaster St. W
Kitchener, ON N2K 1M3
(519) 743-4331
www.lancsmokehouse.com

Taco Farm
Est. 2013
8 Erb St. W
Waterloo, ON N2L 1S7
(519) 208-1300
www.tacofarm.ca

LONDON, ON
The Bungalow
Est. 2009
910 Waterloo St.
London, ON N6A 3W9
(519) 434-8797
www.bungalowhub.ca

The Early Bird
Est. 2012
355 Talbot St.
London, ON N6A 2R5
(519) 439-6483
www.theearlybird.ca

Prince Albert's Diner
Est. 1985
565 Richmond St.
London, ON N6A 3G2
(519) 432-2835

MONTREAL, QC
Brit & Chips
Est. 2010
5536 chemin de la Côte-des-Neiges
Montreal, QC H3T 1Y8
(514) 737-9555
www.britandchips.com

Burger Bar
Est. 2011
1465 rue Crescent
Montreal, QC H3G 2B2
(514) 903-5575
www.montrealburger.com

Cacao 70
Est. 2011
2087 rue Sainte-Catherine O
Montreal, QC H3H 1M6
(514) 933-1688
www.cacao70.ca

Chez Claudette
Est. 1983
351 avenue Laurier E
Montreal, QC H2T 1G7
(514) 279-5173
www.restaurantchezclaudette.com

Icehouse
Est. 2011
51 rue Roy E
Montreal, QC H2W 2S3
(514) 439-6691

L'Avenue
Est. 1994
922 avenue du Mont-Royal E
Montreal, QC H2J 1X1
(514) 523-8780
www.restaurantlavenue.ca

Léché Desserts
Est. 2012
640 rue de Courcelle
Montreal, QC H4C 3C5
(514) 805-5600
www.lechedesserts.com

The Main Deli Steak House
Est. 1974
3864 boulevard Saint-Laurent
Montreal, QC H2W 1Y2
(514) 843-8126
www.maindelisteakhouse.com

Pizzeria Napoletana
Est. 1948
189 rue Dante
Montreal, QC H2S 1K1
(514) 276-8226
www.napoletana.com

Poutineville
Est. 2010
1365 rue Ontario E
Montreal, QC H2L 1S1
(514) 419-5444
www.poutineville.com

Prohibition
5700 avenue de Monkland
Montreal, QC H4A 1E4
(514) 481-8466
www.prohibitionmontreal.com

Satay Brothers
Est. 2011
3721 rue Notre-Dame O
Montreal, QC H4C 1P8
(514) 933-3507

❏ Schwartz's Deli
Est. 1928
3895 boulevard Saint-Laurent
Montreal, QC H2W 1X9
(514) 842-4813
www.schwartzsdeli.com

MONT-TREMBLANT, QC
❏ Crêperie Catherine
Est. 1995
977 rue Labelle
Mont-Tremblant, QC J8E 2W5
(819) 681-4888
www.creperiecatherine.ca

ORANGEVILLE, ON
❏ Barb's Country Kitchen
Est. 2013
634041 Highway 10
Orangeville, ON L9W2Z1
(519) 938-8282

❏ Barley Vine Rail Company
Est. 2013
35 Armstrong St.
Orangeville, ON L9W 3H6
(519) 942-3400
www.thebvrco.com

❏ Philadelphia Kitchen
Est. 2011
281 Broadway Ave.
Orangeville, ON L9W 1L2
(519) 938-8970
www.philadelphiakitchen.ca

❏ Soulyve
Est. 2009
34 Mill St.
Orangeville, ON L9W 2M3
(519) 307-5983
www.soulyve.ca

ORILLIA, ON
❏ Tre Sorelle
Est. 2004
133 Mississauga St. E
Orillia, ON L3V 5A9
(705) 325-8507
www.tresorelleorillia.com

OTTAWA, ON
❏ Art-Is-In Boulangerie
Est. 2006
250 City Centre Ave., #112
Ottawa, ON K1R 1C7
(613) 695-1226
www.artisinbakery.com

❏ Burgers 'n' Fries Forever
Est. 2013
329 Bank St.
Ottawa, ON K2P 1X9
(613) 230-3456
www.burgersnfriesforever.com

❏ El Camino
Est. 2013
380 Elgin St.
Ottawa, ON K2P 1N1
(613) 422-2800
www.eatelcamino.com

❏ Elgin Street Diner
Est. 1993
374 Elgin St.
Ottawa, ON K2P 1N1
(613) 237-9700
www.elginstreetdiner.com

❏ The Manx
Est. 1993
370 Elgin St.
Ottawa, ON K2P 1N1
(613) 231.2070
www.manxpub.com

❏ Pressed
Est. 2011
750 Gladstone Ave.
Ottawa, ON K1R 6X5
(613) 680-9294
www.pressed-ottawa.com

❏ The SmoQue Shack
Est. 2011
129 York St.
Ottawa, ON K1N 5T4
(613) 789-4245
www.smoqueshack.com

❏ Stoneface Dolly's
Est. 1995
416 Preston St.
Ottawa, ON K1S 4M9
(613) 564-2222
www.stonefacedollys.com

❏ Two Six {Ate}
Est. 2012
268 Preston St.
Ottawa, ON K1R 7R3
(613) 695-8200
www.twosixate.com

❏ Wilf & Ada's
Est. 2014 (formally Ada's Diner 1994)
510 Bank St.
Ottawa, ON K2P 1Z4
(613) 231-7959
www.wilfandadas.com

PETERBOROUGH, ON
❏ Reggie's Hot Grill
Est. 2007
89 Hunter St. E
Peterborough, ON K9H 1G4
(705) 874-1471
www.reggieshotgrill.ca

❏ Two Dishes Cookshop
Est. 2014
261 Charlotte St.
Peterborough, ON K9J 2V3
(705) 775-2650
www.twodishescookshop.tumblr.com

QUEBEC CITY, QC
❏ Casa Calzone
Est. 2000
1298 rue de la Pointe-aux-Lièvres
Quebec City, QC G1L 4L9
(418) 522-3000
www.casacalzone.com

❏ Le Chic Shack
Est. 2012
15 rue du Fort
Quebec City, QC G1R 3W9
(418) 692-1485
www.lechicshack.ca

SAULT STE. MARIE, ON
❏ Ernie's Coffee Shop
Est. 1950
13 Queen St. E
Sault Ste. Marie, ON P6A 1Y4
(705) 253-9216

❏ Low & Slow
Est. 2014
480 Albert St. W
Sault Ste. Marie, ON P6A 1C3
(705) 450-6328
www.eatlownslow.com

**ST. CATHARINES, ON, AND
SURROUNDING AREA**
❏ August Restaurant
Est. 2008
5204 King St.
Beamsville, ON L0R 1B3
(905) 563-0200
www.augustrestaurant.ca

❏ The Bull BBQ Pit
Est. 2011
24 St Paul St.
St. Catharines, ON L2R 3M2
(905) 397-3287
www.thebullbbqpit.com

❏ The Garrison House
Est. 2012
111C Garrison Village Dr., #2
Niagara-on-the-Lake, ON L0S 1J0
(905) 468-4000
www.thegarrisonhouse.ca

❏ Joe Feta's Greek Village
Est. 1995
290 Lake St.
St. Catharines, ON L2N 4H5
(905) 646-3399
www.joefetas.ca

STRATFORD, ON
❏ Boomers Gourmet Fries
Est. 1998
26 Erie St.
Stratford, ON N5A 1B2
(519) 275-3147
www.boomersgourmetfries.com

THUNDER BAY, ON

❑ **Hoito Restaurant**
Est. 1918
314 Bay St.
Thunder Bay, ON P7B 1S1
(807) 345-6323
www.thehoito.ca

TORONTO, ON

❑ **5 Doors North**
Est. 1997
2088 Yonge St.
Toronto, ON M4S 2A3
(416) 480-6234
www.fivedoorsnorth.com

❑ **Banh Mi Boys**
Est. 2011
392 Queen St. W
Toronto, ON M5V 2A6
(416) 363-0588
www.banhmiboys.com

❑ **Barque Smokehouse**
Est. 2011
299 Roncesvalles Ave.
Toronto, ON M6R 2M3
(416) 532-7700
www.barque.ca

❑ **Beast**
Est. 2010
96 Tecumseth St.
Toronto, ON M6J 2H1
(647) 352-6000
www.thebeastrestaurant.com

❑ **The Borough**
Est. 2014
1352 Danforth Ave.
Toronto, ON M4J 1M9
(416) 901-1429
www.borough.ca

❑ **The Burger's Priest**
Est. 2010
3397 Yonge St.
Toronto, ON M4N 2M7
(416) 488-3510
www.theburgerspriest.com

❑ **Café Polonez**
Est. 1978
195 Roncesvalles Ave.
Toronto, ON M6R 2L5
(416) 532-8432
www.cafepolonez.ca

❑ **Cardinal Rule**
Est. 2011
5 Roncesvalles Ave.
Toronto, ON M6R 2K2
(647) 352-0202
www.cardinalrulerestaurant.com

❑ **Caplansky's**
Est. 2009
356 College St.
Toronto, ON M5T 1S6
(416) 500-3852
www.caplanskys.com

❑ **Casa Manila**
Est. 2010
879 York Mills Rd.
Toronto, ON M3B 1Y5
(416) 443-9654
www.casamanila.ca

❑ **Chino Locos**
Est. 2008
4 Greenwood Ave.
Toronto, ON M4L 2P4
(647) 345-5626
www.chinolocos.com

❑ **The Clubhouse Sandwich Shop**
Est. 2013
455 Spadina Ave.
Toronto, ON M5S 2G8
(647) 502-1291

❑ **The Combine Eatery**
Est. 2011
162 Danforth Ave.
Toronto, ON M4K 1N2
(416) 792-8088
www.thecombineeatery.com

Dr. Laffa
Est. 2011 (relocated 2014)
3027 Bathurst St.
North York, ON M6B 3B5
(647) 352-9000
www.drlaffa.com

El Rincon
Est. 2003
653 St. Clair Ave. W
Toronto, ON M6C 1A7
(416) 656-1059
www.elrinconmexicano.ca

Emma's Country Kitchen
Est. 2012
810 St. Clair Ave. W
Toronto, ON M6E 1A7
(416) 652-3662
www.emmascountrykitchen.com

Fancy Franks
Est. 2012
326 College St.
Toronto, ON M5T 1S3
(416) 920-3647
www.fancyfranks.com

The Gabardine
Est. 2010
372 Bay St.
Toronto, ON M5H 2W9
(647) 352-3211
www.thegabardine.com

Hogtown Smoke
Est. 2011
1959 Queen St. E
Toronto, ON M4L 1H7
(416) 691-9009
www.hogtownsmoke.ca

The Hogtown Vegan
Est. 2011
1056 Bloor St. W
Toronto, ON M6H 1M3
(416) 901-9779
www.hogtownvegan.com

Kinton Ramen
Est. 2012
668 Bloor St. W
Toronto, ON M6G 1L2
(416) 551-8177
www.kintonramen.com

La Cubana
Est. 2013
392 Roncesvalles Ave.
Toronto, ON M6R 2M9
(416) 538-7500
www.lacubana.ca

Lahore Tikka House
Est. 1996
1365 Gerrard St. E
Toronto, ON M4L 1Z3
(416) 406-1668
www.lahoretikkahouse.com

Lisa Marie
Est. 2013
638 Queen St. W
Toronto, ON M6J 1E4
(647) 748-6822
www.fidelgastros.com

Little Fin
Est. 2014
4 Temperance St.
Toronto, ON M5H 1Y5
(647) 348-7000
www.littlefin.ca

Loaded Pierogi
Est. 2014
1044 Gerrard St. E
Toronto, ON M4M 1Z8
(647) 348-0088
www.loadedpierogi.ca

Mezes
Est. 1996
456 Danforth Ave.
Toronto, ON M4K 1P3
(416) 778-5150
www.mezes.com

❏ Pizzeria Defina
Est. 2011
321 Roncesvalles Ave.
Toronto, ON M6R 2M6
(416) 534-4414
www.pizzeriadefina.com

❏ Pizzeria Via Mercanti
Est. 2006
188 Augusta Ave.
Toronto, ON M5T 1M1
(647) 343-6647
www.pizzeriaviamercanti.ca

❏ Sanremo Bakery
Est. 1969
374 Royal York Rd.
Toronto ON M8Y 2R3
(416) 255-2808
www.sanremobakery.com

❏ Saturday Dinette
Est. 2014
807 Gerrard St. E
Toronto, ON M4M 1Y5
(416) 465-5959
www.saturdaydinette.com

❏ The Senator
Est. 1948
249 Victoria St.
Toronto, ON M5B 1V8
(416) 364-7517
www.thesenator.com

❏ Sky Blue Sky Sandwich Company
Est. 2009
605 Bloor St. W
Toronto, ON M6G 1K6
(647) 351-7945
www.sbssandwiches.com

❏ Tich
Est. 2014
2314 Lake Shore Blvd. W
Etobicoke, ON M8V 1B5
(647) 349-8424
www.tich.ca

❏ Uncle Betty's Diner
Est. 2011
2590 Yonge St.
Toronto, ON M4P 2J3
(416) 483-2590
www.unclebettys.com

❏ Von Doughnuts
Est. 2013
713 Danforth Ave.
Toronto, ON M4J 1L2
(416) 901-8663

❏ The White Brick Kitchen
Est. 2012
641 Bloor St. W
Toronto, ON M6G 1K9
(647) 347-9188
www.thewhitebrickkitchen.com

❏ The Wren
Est. 2013
1382 Danforth Ave.
Toronto, ON M4J 1M9
(647) 748-1382
www.thewrendanforth.com

WINDSOR, ON
❏ Bubi's Awesome Eats
Est. 1977
620 University Ave. W
Windsor, ON N9A 5R5
(519) 252-2001
www.bubis.org

❏ Mamo Burger Bar
Est. 2013
13430 Tecumseh Rd. E
Windsor, ON N8N 2L9
(519) 735-3999
www.mamoburgerbar.com

❏ Motor Burger
Est. 2009
888 Erie St. E
Windsor, ON N9A 3Y9
(519) 252-8004
www.motorburger.ca

❑ Rino's Kitchen
Est. 2010
131 Elliott St. W
Windsor, ON N9A 4N4
(519) 962-8843
www.rinoskitchen.com

❑ Smoke & Spice Southern Barbeque
Est. 2008
7470 Tecumseh Rd. E
Windsor, ON N8T 1E9
(519) 252-4999
www.smokenspice.com

❑ The Twisted Apron
Est. 2011
1833 Wyandotte St. E
Windsor, ON N8Y 1E2
(519) 256-2665
www.thetwistedapron.com

EASTERN CANADA

CAPE BRETON ISLAND, NS, AND SURROUNDING AREA
❑ Charlene's Bayside Restaurant and Cafe
Est. 2008
9657 Highway 105
Whycocomagh, NS B0E 3M0
(902) 756-8004

❑ Colette's Place
Est. 1982
201 Brookside St.
Glace Bay, NS B1A 1L6
(902) 849-8430

❑ Flavor 19
Est. 2011
Lingan Golf Course
1225 Grand Lake Rd.
Sydney, NS B1M 1A2
(905) 562-2233
www.cbflavor.com/nineteen

CHARLOTTETOWN, PEI
❑ The Churchill Arms
Est. 2003
75 Queen St.
Charlottetown, PEI C1A 4A8
(902) 367-3450
www.churchillarms.ca

❑ Famous Peppers
Est. 2003 (relocated 2011)
202 Kent St.
Charlottetown, PEI C1A 1P2
(902) 370-7070
www.famouspeppers.ca

❑ Water-Prince Corner Shop and Lobster Pound
Est. 1991
141 Water St.
Charlottetown, PEI C1A 1A8
(902) 368-3212
www.waterprincelobster.ca

HALIFAX, NS
❑ 2 Doors Down
Est. 2013
1533 Barrington St.
Halifax, NS B3J 3X7
(902) 422-4224
www.go2doorsdown.com

❑ The Armview Restaurant & Lounge
Est. 1951
7156 Chebucto Rd.
Halifax, NS B3L 1N4
(905) 455-4395
www.thearmview.com

❑ Boneheads BBQ
Est. 2010
1014 Barrington St.
Halifax, NS B3H 2P9
(902) 407-4100
www.lickthebone.com

❑ Hali Deli
Est. 2011
2389 Agricola St.
Halifax, NS B3K 4B8
(902) 406-2500
www.halideli.com

❏ Morris East
Est. 2007
5212 Morris St.
Halifax, NS B3J 1B4
(902) 444-7663
www.morriseast.com

❏ Salvatore's Pizzaiolo Trattoria
Est. 1994
5541 Young St.
Halifax, NS B3K 1Z7
(902) 455-1133
www.salvatorespizza.ca

LUNENBURG, NS
❏ Magnolia's Grill
Est. 1987
128 Montague St.
Lunenburg, NS B0J 2C0
(902) 634-3287
www.magnolias-grill.com

❏ Salt Shaker Deli
Est. 2006
124 Montague St.
Lunenburg, NS B0J 2C0
(902) 640-3434
www.saltshakerdeli.com

MONCTON, NB
❏ Catch 22 Lobster Bar
Est. 2011
589 Main St.
Moncton, NB E1C 1C6
(506) 855-5335
www.catch22lobsterbar.com

❏ Tide & Boar Gastropub
Est. 2011
700 Main St.
Moncton, NB E1C 1E4
(506) 857-9118
www.tideandboar.com

PETTY HARBOUR, NL
❏ Chafe's Landing
Est. 2008
11 Main Rd., Petty Harbour
St. John's, NL A0A 3H0
(709) 747-0802
www.chafeslanding.com

SAINT JOHN, NB
❏ Saint John Ale House
Est. 2003
1 Market Sq.
Saint John, NB E2L 4Z6
(506) 657-2337
www.saintjohnalehouse.com

❏ Taco Pica Restaurant
Est. 1993
96 Germain St.
Saint John, NB E2L 2E7
(506) 633-8492
www.tacopica.ca

❏ Urban Deli
Est. 2009
68 King St.
Saint John, NB E2L 1G4
(506) 652-3354
www.urbandeli.ca

ST. JOHN'S, NL
❏ Ches's Famous Fish & Chips
Est. 1951
9 Freshwater Rd.
St. John's, NL A1C 2N1
(709) 726-2373
www.chessfishandchips.ca

❏ Piatto Pizzeria
Est. 2010
377 Duckworth St.
St. John's, NL A1C 1H8
(709) 726-0909
www.piattopizzeria.com

❏ Rocket Bakery and Fresh Food
Est. 2011
272 Water St.
St. John's, NL A1C 1B7
(709) 738-2011
www.rocketfood.ca

❏ YellowBelly Brewery
Est. 2008
288 Water St.
St. John's, NL A1C 5J9
(709) 757-3784
www.yellowbellybrewery.com

ST. PETER'S BAY, PEI
❑ Rick's Fish 'n' Chips &
 Seafood House
Est. 1992
5544 Route 2
St. Peter's Bay, PEI C1A 2A0
(902) 961-3438
www.ricksfishnchips.com

SUSSEX, NB
❑ Gasthof Old Bavarian Restaurant
Est. 1985
1130 Knightville Rd.
Sussex, NB E4G 1E7
(506) 433-4735
www.oldbavarian.ca

VICTORIA-BY-THE-SEA, PEI
❑ Landmark Café
Est. 1989
12 Main St.
Victoria-by-the-Sea, PEI C0A 2G0
(902) 658-2286
www.landmarkcafe.ca

NORTHERN CANADA

WHITEHORSE, YT
❑ Antoinette's Food Cache
Est. 2006
4121 4th Ave.
Whitehorse, YT Y1A 1H7
(867) 668-3505
www.antoinettesfoodcache.ca

❑ Klondike Rib & Salmon
Est. 1994
2116 2nd Ave.
Whitehorse, YT Y1A 1B9
(867) 667-7554
www.klondikerib.com

UNITED STATES

AUSTIN, TX
❑ Mi Madre's
Est. 1990
2201 Manor Rd.
Austin, TX 78722
(512) 322-9721
www.mimadresrestaurant.com

❑ Noble Sandwich
Est. 2010
12233 Ranch Rd. 620 N, #105
Austin, TX 78750
(512) 382-6248
www.noblesandwiches.com

BOSTON, MA
❑ Saus
Est. 2010
33 Union St.
Boston, MA 02108
(617) 248-8835
www.sausboston.com

BUFFALO, NY
❑ Fat Bob's Smokehouse
Est. 1999
41 Virginia Pl.
Buffalo, NY 14202
(716) 887-2971
www.fatbobs.com

CAMBRIDGE, MA
❑ Frank's Steakhouse
Est. 1938
2310 Massachusetts Ave.
North Cambridge, MA 02140
(617) 661-0666
www.frankssteakhouse.com

CHICAGO, IL
❑ Lou Malnati's
Est. 1971
1120 North State St.
Chicago, IL 60610
(312) 725-7777
www.loumalnatis.com

❑ **Manny's Cafeteria and Delicatessen**
Est. 1942
1141 South Jefferson St.
Chicago, IL 60607
(312) 939-2855
www.mannysdeli.com

CLEVELAND, OH
❑ **Happy Dog at the Euclid Tavern**
Est. 2009
11625 Euclid Ave.
Cleveland, OH 44106
(216) 231-5400
www.happydogcleveland.com

❑ **Sweet Moses**
Est. 2011
6800 Detroit Ave.
Cleveland, OH 44102
(216) 651-2202
www.sweetmosestreats.com

MEMPHIS, TN
❑ **Kooky Canuck**
Est. 2005
87 South 2nd St.
Memphis, TN 38103
(901) 578-9800
www.kookycanuck.com

❑ **Payne's Bar-B-Que**
Est. 1972
1762 Lamar Ave.
Memphis, TN 38114
(901) 272-1523

MIAMI, FL
❑ **11th Street Diner**
Est. in Pennsylvania 1948; in Miami 1992
1065 Washington Ave.
Miami Beach, FL 33139
(305) 534-6373
www.eleventhstreetdiner.com

❑ **El Mago de las Fritas**
Est. 1983
5828 Southwest 8th St.
West Miami, FL 33144
(305) 266-8486
www.elmagodelasfritas.com

❑ **La Camaronera Seafood Joint and Fish Market**
Est. 1966
1952 West Flagler St.
Miami, FL 33135
(305) 642-3322
www.lacamaronera.com

NASHVILLE, TN, AND SURROUNDING AREA
Edley's Bar-B-Que
Est. 2011
2706 12th Ave. S
Nashville, TN 37204
(615) 953-2951
www.edleysbbq.com

❑ **The Loveless Cafe**
Est. 1951
8400 Tennessee Highway 100
Nashville, TN 37221
(615) 646-9700
www.lovelesscafe.com

❑ **Puckett's**
Est. 1998
120 4th Ave. S
Franklin, TN 37064
(615) 794-5527
www.puckettsgro.com

NEW ORLEANS, LA
❑ **Dreamy Weenies**
Est. 2012
740 North Rampart St.
New Orleans, LA 70116
(504) 872-0157
www.dreamyweenies.com

❑ **Katie's**
Est. 1984
3701 Iberville St.
New Orleans, LA 70119
(504) 488-6582
www.katiesinmidcity.com

❑ **Parkway Bakery & Tavern**
Est. 1911/2003
538 Hagan Ave.
New Orleans, LA 70119
(504) 482-3047
www.parkwaypoorboys.com

PORTLAND, OR
❑ Lardo
Est. 2010
1212 Southeast Hawthorne Blvd.
Portland, OR 97214
(503) 234-7786
www.lardosandwiches.com

❑ Shut Up and Eat
Est. 2010
3848 SE Gladstone St.
Portland, OR 97202
(503) 719-6449
www.shutupandeatpdx.com

❑ Tilt
Est. 2011
1355 Northwest Everett St., #120
Portland, OR 97209
(503) 894-9528
www.tiltitup.com

SEATTLE, WA
❑ Porkchop & Co.
Est. 2014
5451 Leary Ave.
Seattle, WA 98107
(206) 257-5761
www.eatatporkchop.com

❑ Queen Bee Cafe
Est. 2014
2200 East Madison St., Ste. B
Seattle, WA 98112
(206) 757-6314
www.queenbeecafe.com

TUCSON, AZ
❑ Baja Café
Est. 2014
7002 East Broadway Blvd.
Tucson, AZ 85710
(520) 495-4772
www.bajacafetucson.com

❑ BOCA Tacos y Tequila
Est. 2010
828 East Speedway Blvd.
Tucson, AZ 85719
(520) 777-8134
www.bocatacos.com

❑ Mother Hubbard's Cafe
Est. 1973
14 West Grant Rd.
Tucson, AZ 85705
(520) 623-7976
www.motherhubbardscafe.com

INTERNATIONAL

DUBLIN, IRELAND
❑ Gallagher's Boxty House
Est. 1990
20-21 Temple Bar
Dublin 2, Ireland
(+353) 1 677 2762
www.boxtyhouse.ie

❑ L. Mulligan Grocer
Est. 1790
18 Stoneybatter
Dublin 7, Ireland
(+353) 1 670 9889
www.lmulligangrocer1.weebly.com

❑ Oar House Restaurant
Est. 2003
8 West Pier, Howth
Dublin, Ireland
(+353) 1 839 4562
www.oarhouse.ie

FLORENCE, ITALY
❑ All'Antico Vinaio
Est. 1995
Via dei Neri 74 R
50122 Florence, Italy
(+39) 055 238 2723
www.allanticovinaio.com

❑ Trattoria Mario
Est. 1953
Via Rosina 2 R
50123 Florence, Italy
(+39) 055 218550
www.trattoria-mario.com

❏ **Trattoria 4 Leoni**
Est. 1995
Via dei Vellutini 1 R
50125 Florence, Italy
(+39) 055 218562
www.4leoni.com

ROME, ITALY
❏ **Flavio al Velavevodetto**
Est. 2007
Via di Monte Testaccio 97
00153 Rome, Italy
(+39) 06 5744194
www.ristorantevelavevodetto.it

❏ **La Gatta Mangiona**
Est. 1999
Via Federico Ozanam 30-32
00152 Rome, Italy
(+39) 06 534 6702
www.lagattamangiona.com

❏ **Tonda**
Est. 2011
Via Valle Corteno 31
00141 Rome, Italy
(+39) 06 818 0960

LONDON, UK
❏ **The Princess Victoria**
Est. 2011
217 Uxbridge Rd.
London, UK W12 9DH
(+44) 20 8749 5886
www.princessvictoria.co.uk

❏ **Roti Chai**
Est. 2011
3 Portman Mews S
London, UK W1H 6HS
(+44) 20 7408 0101
www.rotichai.com

❏ **The Mayfair Chippy**
Est. 2014
14 North Audley St.
London, UK W1K 6WE
(+44) 20 7741 2233
www.mayfairchippy.com